Released from
Samford University Library

CORWIN
PRESS

The Corwin Press logo—a raven striding across an open book—represents the happy union of courage and learning. We are a professional-level publisher of books and journals for K-12 educators, and we are committed to creating and providing resources that embody these qualities. Corwin's motto is "Success for All Learners."

Parents Are Lifesavers

A Handbook for Parent Involvement in Schools

Carol S. Batey

CORWIN PRESS, INC.
A Sage Publications Company
Thousand Oaks, California

Samford University Library

Copyright © 1996 by Corwin Press, Inc.

All rights reserved. No part of this book may be reproduced or utilized in any form or by any means, electronic or mechanical, including photocopying, recording, or by any information storage and retrieval system, without permission in writing from the publisher.

For information address:

Corwin Press, Inc.
A Sage Publications Company
2455 Teller Road
Thousand Oaks, California 91320
E-mail: order@corwin.sagepub.com

SAGE Publications Ltd.
6 Bonhill Street
London EC2A 4PU
United Kingdom

SAGE Publications India Pvt. Ltd.
M-32 Market
Greater Kailash I
New Delhi 110 048 India

Printed in the United States of America

Library of Congress Cataloging-in-Publication Data

Batey, Carol S.
     Parents are lifesavers: A handbook for parent involvement in
schools / author, Carol S. Batey.
          p. cm.
     Includes bibliographical references and index.
     ISBN 0-8039-6240-1 (cloth: acid-free paper). — ISBN
0-8039-6241-X (pbk.: acid-free paper)
          1. Home and school—United States—Handbooks, manuals, etc.
2. Education—Parent participation—United States—Handbooks,
manuals, etc. I. Title.
     LC225.3B39   1996
     370.19'312—dc20   95-32513

This book is printed on acid-free paper.

96 97 98 99 10 9 8 7 6 5 4 3 2 1

Corwin Press Project Editor: Christina M. Hill

LC
225.3
. B39
1996

Contents

Foreword

Parents may be receiving less help from neighbors and the wider community presently than at most points in history. Indeed, most parents feel they must actively intervene to *counter* the culture their children experience in the community. Indications are that peers and the media are more influential on young people's behavior than 20 years ago and that the family and church are less influential.

Parents Are Lifesavers offers a practical path to new partnerships between schools and parents. Such "lifesaving" partnerships are, in my opinion, essential if both families and schools are to serve our children and our future in the manner needed.

We must all work together if our children are to acquire the knowledge, skills, and character they will need. Our country is one born of ideals. We have national purposes. Schools and parents must join hands if our children are to have the will and the skill to continue that American adventure in liberty and justice.

Richard C. Benjamin, *Director*
Metropolitan Nashville Public Schools

Acknowledgments

I first want to thank my Creator, the inspiration and guide in my life. I feel much gratitude for the sacrifices made by my husband, Joseph, and my six children while I put this book together. Thanks to my mother, Mildred Starks, for being a lifelong educator in our family.

I owe praises to Alice Foster of Corwin Press who encouraged me to develop this handbook for all parents, administrators, teachers, school board members, and community members. It has been accomplished through much teamwork and collaboration. I am also thankful to the parents and students in public schools; without them, this book could not have been written.

A special thanks goes to Betty Triplett, my mentor, and to Grace Jones, Jenny Shuck, Kathy Bishop, and Gloria Sawyers for their editorial assistance and consistent encouragement. I give a big "hat's off" to Dr. Richard C. Benjamin for hiring me as a parent-consultant for the Metropolitan Nashville Public Schools.

Thank you also to my typists and technical assistants, Evan Richards and Karen Cunningham, for their invaluable contribution. Finally, I extend love and warm wishes to *all* who will read this handbook and try to model these examples within their school organizations.

Introduction
Inviting Parents to Participate

As violence and student failures continue to escalate, parent and community involvement is emerging as the vital "missing link" to reaching educational goals in many school communities. On the other hand, knowing how to involve parents remains a big puzzle for many professional educators and parent-leaders.

Parents are often invited to participate in designing parent involvement strategies—after all, parents are the major stakeholders in their children's education. Just as often, however, such efforts fall short of success because the school climate is neither inviting nor appropriately set. Although parental involvement is a widespread concern, not all authorities know how to develop it.

What do schools with high levels of parental involvement do that is different? How can educators encourage parent participation in the home and school? *Parents Are Lifesavers* provides answers in the form of practical, well-defined solutions for educators, parents, and community members. The book offers useful strategies for building effective and long-lasting partnerships.

It begins with a step-by-step model plus an outline to guide anyone seeking direction on how to get parents involved in their children's schools. A "parent involvement improvement contract" is also provided to assist readers in recommitting to their own involvement with parents.

About the Chapters

Chapter 1 tells my own history, first as a parent volunteer and then as someone actively involved with the school system. This chapter reveals how and why I made the decision to serve and how I persevered with confidence. For example, every new parent-president of a parent-teacher or parent group starts with a flood of emotion to overcome. The primary emotions I felt were doubt, fear, and happiness. There were many challenges to face, including the mind-set of teachers and the economic status of our organization. Nevertheless, as copresident, I took the initiative to honor the Swahili word, *Harambee:* "Let's pull together." I attribute the success of the program to the teamwork of all stakeholders and to the inspiration and vision of Betty Triplett, principal of Napier Primary School, an inner-city school in our community.

Chapter 2 details methods for creating a context for parent participation. Effective strategies must include more than the use of a survey or a note sent home asking parents to volunteer. This chapter gives examples of how to extend an invitation to parents. Educators and parent-leaders can strengthen home and school relationships with this practical, hands-on information based on the experience I acquired working in the field of parent involvement.

Chapter 3 examines the networking process. Every successful parent-teacher group begins by effectively organizing a volunteer network. Networking is, in reality, sharing information. A parent-teacher association (PTA) or parent-teacher organization (PTO) runs smoothly when volunteer parents work together and learn to exchange information and acknowledge each other's strength.

Chapter 4 focuses on gaining the benefit of parents' knowledge and experience in the school and at home. This chapter begins with Dr. Joyce Epstein's (1993) identification of the five types of parental involvement, based on her research at the Johns Hopkins University. These types are volunteering, parenting, communicating, learning at home, and representing other parents. Included is a model of a special education parent involvement association.

Chapter 5 highlights a few Nashville principals who have successfully created strategies for parent participation. These principals have applied for and received both public and nonprofit community funding from the Metropolitan Nashville Public Education Foundation to strengthen the parent connection with their respective schools. As a result, the professionals at each school have been able to provide services such as transportation, visitation, homework assistance, and parent training for families.

It works! It works! Chapter 6 focuses on the outcome of efforts to involve parents and their abilities. Case examples explore how parents have participated hand in hand with the district school system, especially in situations in which the community was required to meet a crisis or provide a safer school atmosphere.

A Plan to
Action Improvement Plan

For your school or organization to be effective in parent and community involvement, clarification is needed for three terms used in this book—*mission, vision,* and *plan to action.* According to the dictionary, a mission is a certain task to be carried out to produce a desired outcome. The ideal task of parent-teacher groups is to form true "village" partnerships for student achievement. These relationships between the community, staff, students, and parents should be created without regard for one's race, creed, gender, exceptionality, or social or economic status. The result will be a better and stronger village for all villagers.

A vision is important to every parent-teacher group. After the mission has been well-defined, the group leaders and members will need a vision for developing an effective mission. What steps are needed to complete the task at hand? Specifically, decisions will have to be made about how parents and community volunteers can support the school and enhance students' learning. Principals and parent-leaders must be visionary chiefs in their important mission. Use your imagination to tap into and make use of the power of parents and community members. Many within the school setting are willing to give to your school. Someone must make the effort and take the time to reach out to them. Many parents feel they are not a part of the school's village. Yet the African proverb states, "It takes a whole village to educate a child." In our organizations, what have we been missing?

Finally, a plan to action must be clarified to provide a method for achieving your goals. When designing your group's action plan, consider the following:

- Start with a small representation of students, parents, community members, and educators.
- Get opinions from the entire parent-teacher body. This input is important for an assessment.
- Specify the steps to be taken in carrying out a plan to action. Clarify who will help complete each step and how much time it will take to complete. An example follows.

Plan to Action

Job	Time	Name
1. To find parents willing to work on calendar committee	August 1 to August 15 Report to Steering Committee by August 15, 1995 at 6 p.m.	John Doe

Parent Involvement Improvement Contract

Educators, parent-leaders, and community members: Please list ways you know to increase the involvement of your parents. You are invited to start a plan to action so you can improve your commitment to parent involvement.

After you've read this book, answer the following questions to help determine your commitment as a volunteer. Following the questions is a "contract" that you can sign and date as a first step in your becoming a parent-volunteer.

1. How can you use the principles taught in Chapter 1 to increase parent activity in the classroom and at school? Write your mission statement for parent involvement.
2. What have you learned that you could implement tomorrow?
3. How can you prepare to remove the invisible and visible walls of opposition that affect your school's parent involvement.
4. How can you best use parents' and students' expertise in your group or classroom?
5. Do you believe that parents are lifesavers? Explain why or why not.
6. What ideas did you get from any of the chapters to increase your partnerships with the parents you serve?
7. List how educators, parents, and community members can make a difference together.
8. How can you improve participation with non-English-speaking families?

I, _____, believe that parents are lifesavers. I pledge to strengthen my partnership with children's learning.

Date _____

About the Author

Carol Batey is the founder of Batey and Associates, a firm committed to disseminating information about parent involvement in schools and providing seminars for educators, parents, and other interested citizens in the community. She is also the Parent Involvement Consultant for the Metropolitan Nashville Public Schools in Tennessee and has received nationwide recognition from educators for her work on parent involvement. She was educated in the Nashville public schools system, obtained an Associate Degree in business from Falls Business College, and has studied at Tennessee State University and Volunteer State College. In 1991, she and her husband, Joseph, were elected as copresidents of the parent-teacher club at the inner-city school where their six children have been bused while in the primary grades. During the school year, she was nominated for the J. C. Penney Golden Rule Award and won $1,000 for the school. This award is given to individuals who have performed outstanding service to the local community.

1 My Journey to Parent Involvement

I don't type. I don't bake cupcakes. I don't have a degree. I don't even have a child in school; but listen carefully. I want to make a difference. There must be things that I can't see. So I close my eyes and think about what a child explained to me. Parents are lifesavers when a child sails a stormy sea, a helping hand can fill a sail. A smile sets you sailing peacefully. And take a look inside for gifts that hide—it's not too hard to see. Parents Are Lifesavers, and what they share is that they care for you and me.

—From the song "Parents Are Lifesavers," by
Andrew Dunn, music teacher at Stratton
Elementary School, Nashville, Tennessee.
(Copyright 1993. Used with permission.)

Educators, parent-leaders, and community members, let me take you on the journey of my own parent leadership within my children's school. This journey will encompass fears, challenges, insights, struggles, and a "plan to action" necessary for a successful and functioning parent-teacher group.

My story began at Napier Primary School located in the inner city between two drug-infested housing projects. Although these areas have high levels of crime, lots of good people live within them.

Principal Betty Triplett had worked very hard for several years to lay a solid foundation for parent participation at Napier. She was open to any parent who entered the school building. But most of the parent-leaders and volunteers were of only one color. It was her desire to offer invitations to *all* of the parents to share in the yearlong calendar and be part of a steering committee.

The first year my child entered the school, I asked the principal to remove my child from a certain teacher's room because I had a problem. Her response was "No"; however, I didn't give up. Then she said, "Yes," but only if I would volunteer. I said that of course I would, and I worked very hard to be a positive influence on the parents and teachers.

The next year, I had three children attending this school. The principal asked me to come by to visit her 2 weeks before school began. When I went to her office, I was amazed at the warmth and love she demonstrated for the students. I was used to a sterile atmosphere and a coldness from the administration that conveyed the message, "I'm in charge." This principal's office was different, and I felt her concern for all families. I said to myself, "I can trust this administrator because she's frank and genuine."

The question came up, "Mrs. Batey, will you and your husband serve as cochairs of our Parent/Teacher Club?" I was astonished and humbled to think they were asking my husband, a railroader, and me, a homemaker. I declined, even though I felt a sense of gratitude. I had been a stay-at-home mom taking care of six children for 8 years. I didn't have a professional wardrobe, and as I saw it, I had no qualifications. In addition, I had a low self-image. I soon learned that this is the same position that many other potential parent-leaders are in, but they keep it to themselves.

I went home and shared this information with my husband. He immediately said, "Carol, you don't have time." I thought about what he said and realized that he was thinking only about the demands of our own household. At this point, I had to make the decision all by myself. What was right for me? I picked up the phone, called Betty Triplett, and said "Yes." Afterward, I went into shock!

This proved to be the right move for my entire family and the school community. My husband ended up supporting all the efforts of Napier's Parent/Teacher Club. My role not only had a positive effect on my life, but it also positively influenced parents who had never been approached to participate in the past. The support my husband and I provided came in many different ways—money, time, and a caring attitude. My children followed suit by making their own peanut butter sandwiches for school lunches and learning to cook hot dogs for dinner. These acts fostered a welcomed sense of independence in them that was truly heartening.

Beginning With a Plan to Action

I then followed the dictates of my heart and the principles in which I deeply believe. My first plan to action came when I to decided to accept a call to serve in the learning community. As I looked up *service* in the dictionary, I read that it means "work done for others." How was I going to follow through with this service? I wondered. I needed to look deep within and examine my motives, my sincerity, and my feeling of self-worth. After all, I was just a mom.

As a parent-leader, you must decide on your level of commitment and what it will take to carry it out. Only you can make this decision. When I examined my inner self, I found huge amounts of fear. I also discovered happiness and a sense of direction that felt as if I were on the right path. I wondered how I could balance this journey with the needs of my large family. I truly wanted to make a difference in the families of the students at Napier. This, for me, was one of the most difficult struggles I had to face and quickly confront.

Just about all of my extended family members have been certified as educators in various school systems. My own mother taught school for 30 years, and there were always educators in my neighborhood and in my home influencing me in one way or another. I had therefore witnessed many of the personal challenges that educators face and knew that they are human beings with weaknesses and strengths like anyone else. Most parent-leaders have not been prepared to see educators simply as people. Even so, I was well aware of the way teachers often view people lacking an educational degree, and I feared their judgments. So I asked myself, "How do *I* want to be treated?" Then, before I began to preside as copresident, I committed to my second plan to action—to treat all people with honesty and respect. This included all parents, educators, students, and community members with whom I would come in contact.

There I was with a ready smile, a ready hug, and acceptance for all. I strove to be a reachable, teachable servant. One teacher

observed, "Mrs. Batey works like a full-time employee of Napier."
Many times I barely had gas money to get to the school. But I was
there daily to implement the plan to action, working day and night,
hard and long. After 2 months of laying the foundation, everything
at home and school was better organized. I didn't have to work as
hard to maintain what was now in place. In the process, I lost 30
pounds and, to my surprise, developed a better self-image and
family image.

My third plan to action originated when I was able to divert the
focus from myself to the concept of servanthood. I was also able to
accept the principal's mission and share her authority. When principals, teachers, and parent-leaders share administrative authority,
everyone is empowered. For example, parent-leaders are frequently
used as a channel to draw parents into school involvement. But it
took the principal of Napier to say, "I want a *true* partnership with
all of my parents, not just a paper commitment. The parents of
Napier are teachers, too. They are important to this school's surroundings, and as such, we must involve them!" She expressed that
the school didn't belong to the teachers, staff, or herself, but it
belonged to the entire community.

The fourth plan to action unfolded as I discovered that a few
leaders were afraid to let go of power and control. Perhaps they
wanted to share power as part of a school improvement plan, but
certain past experiences had made them wary. Take, for example, a
situation in which a parent comes to volunteer and, as a result,
misjudges a sincere teacher's action in the classroom. The parent
takes action and calls the central office of the school board to
complain. The administrative office then calls the local school and
shares the concern with the principal, who in turn confronts the
teacher in question. The teacher may be understandably upset over
what seems an unnecessary, petty complaint. This type of involvement spoils the venue for other parents, teachers, and children to
develop trust, and it becomes an obstacle to the idea of shared
power. Parents need to be certain that they have a legitimate complaint before filing a grievance.

On the other hand, principals and teachers have used parents
to carry out their own hidden agendas. This takes many forms,
such as asking parents to conduct fund-raisers, tell on other teachers, or solicit the central office's attention. Principals should realize

that these actions jeopardize parents who may be willing to serve. Principals, teachers, and parent-leaders should be able to share their administrative power. By doing this, all stakeholders are empowered.

My fifth plan to action was to identify what steps were needed at Napier before total parent involvement could evolve. As I assessed the school's needs and compared them to those of other schools, they seemed overwhelming. Many at this inner-city school had complained for several years that teachers had given up on getting parents in the area involved with the school. I did not want this to shadow my perception, so I changed my own actions. I soon found that it didn't take whips, chains, finger-pointing, or preaching to lift teachers' spirits—just enthusiasm, a positive attitude, and a pleasant personality. It was important, too, to be an exemplary model for those who might feel inner-city parents have nothing to offer. I would advise principals, teachers, and parent-leaders to go above and beyond the call of service, to reach out even to those you perceive have little to offer.

Teachers at inner-city schools have heavy burdens placed on them daily. During my time of service at Napier, the teachers regularly patrolled the playground in search of hypodermic needles discarded by drug users. Teachers were used to doing all the things that members of a parent-volunteer organization might be able to do. After the club was organized, things changed. The vice president was especially concerned about this situation. As she said, along with the principal and myself, "People and groups in communities have particular needs, and they should have the opportunity to express their needs to others." The first step in the overall plan to action was to create a "wish list" to identify and communicate the needs of all stakeholders.

As most educators and parent-leaders know, schools do not have large budgets. Such was the case at Napier. The Parent/Teacher Club account came to only $300. That was all the money allotted to cover many, many needs! The plan to action could not be stymied by this lack of resources. It was necessary to set goals and work toward accomplishment. If I stopped and focused on the fact that there wasn't enough money to meet our needs, we wouldn't have any successes. To solve this major barrier in education, I, like others, had to assess how to handle the situation and then move forward.

Designing a Collaborative Effort

I started by enlisting the support of parents and community members, requesting that they serve as official leaders of the club or as volunteers within the school. When parents, teachers, or community members had constructive concerns, I listened carefully to understand their goals.

Betty Triplett did not want to use door-to-door fund-raisers to raise money because she felt the children would be placed at risk. The vice president and I shared our fears and started bombarding each other with questions. "How are we going to overcome this challenge and become winners?" This personal approach proved to be very productive. Then I thought out loud, "Let's tap into the resources of the media, parents, and the churches to see if we can get them to donate needed supplies and equipment." Public service announcements, a free service to nonprofit organizations, were used to maximize Napier's message.

During my spare time and while driving to and from my children's schools, I went door-to-door to various businesses, hand delivering letters with lists of requested items. This helped get some of our needs met. I also stopped at garage sales to take advantage of bargains for teachers and students. When parents and I were able to walk into classrooms with requested items, teachers were stunned to find their requests had been filled.

I recall telling parents and teachers, "If any child comes to Napier without money for supplies or field trips, this money will be paid by our club or myself. It would be too traumatic if a child were not able to participate. Who would want a child at Napier stigmatized because of lack of money, clothing, or other materials?" Many times before a field trip, I saw teachers take warm clothing out of a clothes closet set aside for children who were inappropriately dressed for the weather. After I realized this was happening, I began to take items from home to add to the closet. (This task is not listed in the job description of a parent-leader or teacher.)

When the parents and I started fulfilling the teachers' "wishes," new respect between teachers and parents flourished. They quickly changed their perceptions of each other. As we set about developing our plan to action at Napier, we all saw how difficult it is to truly educate a child without proper supplies and equipment. Many teachers in public schools throughout the nation have only dreamed of having volunteers for their classrooms, treats for children, extra field trip money, and most of all, available and enthusiastic parents in the schools to serve as good examples for children. Our dreams became a genuine reality at Napier because of this great team effort.

Becoming a Parent-Consultant

I've discovered from being a parent-leader that to bring about change, it's very important to give a full measure of devotion. At the close of the 1992 school year, I was nominated by parents and teachers for the J. C. Penney Golden Rule Award for volunteering in education. Because of the media exposure I received, parents and teachers across the city of Nashville began calling for consultation. They wanted me to share with them my belief that parents are lifesavers in children's education. Most callers were interested in how to get and keep inner-city parents involved. They also wanted to know how to make the most out of parents' talents and asked if I would help them form a parent-teacher group. I felt I had a mission to share and knew how to develop parent-teacher teams based on my successful experiences at Napier. I accepted all invitations, traveling to schools between that August and the following February free of charge, without even gas money. I learned a lot as I shared my "parents are lifesavers" techniques and insights.

When a new school director was appointed in 1992, a new school improvement plan was implemented that stressed the importance of involving the whole community. I attended a public town meeting and was fortunate enough to hear Dr. Richard C. Benjamin, director of the Metropolitan Nashville Public Schools. He spoke about his "Strategic Plan for School Improvement."

During the question-and-answer segment of the meeting, I shared a number of ideas and strategies I had gained from being a volunteer at Napier. I also shared the fact that parents are tired of being used only as fund-raisers, a statement that received a round of applause. Dr. Benjamin was pleased to see these parents respond so favorably to new and much needed ideas.

After the segment was over, I said, "Dr. Benjamin, if you could give me gas money and a small amount of money for expenses, I could continue my work and give you the information."

"There is not a job description like that," he observed.

I replied, "Dr. Benjamin, you are the school director. You have the power to create a job for me. Shall I come and see you?" He said, "Yes."

I wrote him a Parents Are Lifesavers proposal and was hired 3 months later. Subsequently, he also appointed me as parent-consultant in the district. My duties, as Dr. Benjamin had envisioned, were to assist schools in improving parent and community involvement as part of their school improvement plans. I was to work with parents and members of the community who were not traditionally involved in education.

At first, some educators could not, or would not, try to understand the vision, nor did they hear the wake-up call with respect to parents and the community working together with them. They were opposed to my appointment because of "turf issues," such as the fact that I was not a certified teacher and had not completed a college degree, nor was my background in the field of education. A small number of parents also had reservations because my job was appointed. They felt they should have been placed instead of me.

I did not dwell on the negative attitudes; there was no time to waste. Neither did I hide my talents under a bushel. Dr. Benjamin, in defending my appointment, said, "We must build on people's gifts, talents, and strengths. We must allow people to be taught innovative procedures when they are willing to learn."

Broadcasting the Message

Thanks to Dr. Benjamin's constant support, I was able to develop the Parents Are Lifesavers program. I implemented ideas that reached many parents, whether their children attended high school, middle school, elementary school, special education classes, or schools with programs for children whose primary language is not English. Even parents with little or no college education or training were able to participate.

In a strategy development meeting, the Chapter 1 (federal projects) coordinator, the school director and I worked together to focus the mission of involving parents in children's learning. I suggested that a slogan be adopted to emphasize the concept that parents are in charge of their children's education. *Lifesavers* kept coming to mind after having seen successful parent involvement methods in other schools. From those observations, the slogan was born—"Parents Are Lifesavers!"

We decided that using the media was the best way to get our message to the community. Press releases, along with follow-up phone calls to newspapers, radio, and television stations, were made for every Parent Are Lifesavers event. The media were cooperative in providing coverage to let the public and parents know about workshops they could attend. T-shirts, designed with the colorful slogan Parents Are Lifesavers, were a huge success. Educators, parents, and community volunteers wore them proudly. Along with the T-shirts, a song was created—a sort of national anthem on a district level. The song (see the opening quotation for this chapter) is titled "Parents Are Lifesavers" (of course) and was written by Andrew Dunn, a teacher at Stratton Elementary School.

To get the message out, I formed media partnerships with a staff writer of the largest daily newspaper in Nashville and with radio and television personnel. I called them personally, introduced myself, and shared my information. We developed trusting and working relationships. A writer for the newspaper submitted an article about the districtwide mission of the parent-consultant and featured the first school that I officially serviced. When the article appeared, the entire community was alerted to the importance of volunteers in the schools.

With the help of the system's communications director and myself, all radio, television, and community newspapers were enlisted to broadcast the message. All helped—local daily newspapers, an African American weekly, employee-owned newspapers, a local monthly magazine, and numerous suburban publications. The Parents Are Lifesavers program was also featured on radio and television news programs—the word was getting out! The programs and ideas were reaching homes throughout middle Tennessee. With the help of media partnerships and the district's new focus, many schools opened their doors and welcomed their parents for active participation.

Parent involvement has been both a journey of personal growth and fulfillment for me and a testimony to others. Effective parent leadership can be created if one is willing and dedicated. When parent-leaders identify their own areas of personal focus, tap into inner strengths, and decide what they are willing to give, they can find true satisfaction in the call to serve.

Principals must set the atmosphere for parents to share in policy making and school improvement decisions. They should express their views to staff, parents, and students and suggest meaningful ways to involve parents. Parents want to be invited to sit at the decision-making table with educators. Parents want to be involved before policies are made. School superintendents also need to be open to parents' suggestions. They should be reachable and teachable administrators who strive to set an example. If a better school system is desired, students and parents must be involved as well as teachers. It will make the superintendent's job easier.

I'm so glad that Principal Betty Triplett and Director Dr. Richard C. Benjamin were willing to improve parent participation and had ears to hear what parents were saying. Matters that had been ignored in the past by administrators were now attended to by educators willing to listen and act positively. The concept "Let's pull together!" forms a basis for what is needed to create closer working relationships between students, parents, educators, administrators, and community members!

2 Creating a Climate for Parent Participation

It is often a challenge for educators to get parents involved in everyday school activities because of geographical distance, lack of motivation, or lack of communication. Parent-leaders and educators do not always know their options, nor have they developed successful ways for reaching parents. But a high level of involvement is possible. By working together, they can learn to solve the main part of the problem—setting the climate in order to reach *all* parents.

Over several years of teacher in-service, parent workshops, and parent involvement consultations, I kept searching for the "missing links" needed to connect parents as partners in the schools. I came to the conclusion that strategies were needed to locate and identify these links. I participated with principals, staff members, community servers, students, and parents to identify six strategies that have been used successfully in various parent involvement programs. The suggestions that follow can be incorporated at any level of your school's organization:

1. Extend an invitation.
2. Ensure safety.
3. Develop a mission.
4. Empower all parents.
5. Blend diverse interests.
6. Communicate with parents.

To help you assess your school's climate, a survey is included at the end of this chapter.

Extending an Invitation

It is a principal's job to create a climate between faculty and parent groups that lets everyone know parents *are* needed in the school. In this way, all parents will know they are welcome to participate in any area of their child's education. A principal who encounters resistance from faculty or staff must push ahead even so. To ensure a positive climate of expectation, administrators must also explain the school's goals and how parents can help. This straight-forward approach will demonstrate that school leaders believe parents and volunteers can accomplish much together.

All community partners are potential lifesavers in children's learning. For example, many children live with persons other than their biological parents—grandparents, extended family members, foster parents, mentors, buddies, or friends. There are even children who reside in institutions. The word *partner* can cover all types of relationships; any member of a family can be a significant player in the parent-teacher partnership game.

Many schools across this nation hold a variety of formal and informal meetings and workshops, but frequently, there is low attendance. I spoke with a representative who sells educational videotapes on parent involvement and parenting skills. She told me that a school might purchase anywhere from $300 to $800 worth of products. To her distress, she learned that when schools set up the opportunity to view the videos, only one or two parents are likely to attend.

After talking with her, it was apparent to me that the climate had not been set to attract needed parent-partners. But what seemed a simple observation to me was profound to her, a fact she eagerly began to share with her business associates. It is true that we are dealing with very basic concepts here. Nevertheless, you may be surprised how often people are astonished when faced with the obvious!

Countering Resistance

Even after invitations have been extended and a warm climate created by educators, sometimes there is still resistance to programs for parents and students. When situations like this occur (and they often do), there are several ways to keep focused. The plan to action may need to incorporate some ideas for parent-teacher meetings or parent workshops. The following are some possibilities that have proved effective:

- Hold the meetings at a nearby church in the parents' neighborhood.
- Meet with the resident association of the public housing project in a joint effort to get parents' attention and support.
- Load the administration and staff on a school bus and take the meeting to the parents. Use a school bus driver who drives buses in the inner city and who can serve as a liaison between school and parents.
- Lay a foundation by having teachers make home visits shortly after the children get off the school bus. This works because children are very excited about parents meeting their teachers. Use your neighborhood bus drivers to spread the word to parents that their child's teacher will be coming to visit.
- Find a community spokesperson to act as liaison between families and school personnel.
- Make phone calls. If parents do not have a phone, send postcards through the mail and send information via the student to parents.
- Brainstorm in a committee meeting to come up with innovative ideas to reach out to all parents with children at school.
- Be persistent. Don't give in to failure.
- Use the media. Find out which television stations, newspapers, radio stations, and cable networks broadcast public service announcements (PSAs). There is no charge for a PSA; stations are required to give this news to their communities.
- When all else fails, have a big party in the parents' neighborhood. Serve food, offer door prizes, and make sure teachers are present. The key words here are *food* and *door prizes*! You may even consider having music and activities for the children (e.g., face painting, fishing for prizes, etc.).

Build on the interest of those who attend parent-oriented functions. Using a needs assessment, find out the favorite interests and skills of their families. Then invite them to share this information in a small-group workshop. You might use one of the following approaches:

- Enlist parents to be leaders in their neighborhoods. The parents will be able to talk with their peers to enhance involvement within the school setting.
- If your school doesn't have parents who would like to represent other parents or form an outreach program, ask a neighborhood church pastor or member to act as a liaison to parents in his or her church.

Helping Parents Feel Welcome

When I was a school volunteer, a teacher once misjudged my actions and I felt victimized. I also felt personally threatened that I was not welcome. The teacher told me that I needed to focus on my own children and stop volunteering. I tried to explain my actions, and the next day I reported this mistake to the administration of the school. No action was taken; my complaint was not even acknowledged. The principal lacked experience and was not willing to get involved or recognize the emotional pain I felt. I did not enter my child's homeroom for the remainder of the school year. It was also hard for me to visit the school or volunteer for anything else.

The *New Webster's Dictionary* (Bolander & Stodden, 1986) defines *safe* as "free from danger, unhurt, secure, involving no danger or risk." A parent must feel a sense of psychological security to enter the school's doors to volunteer or to be part of an audience.

Here are some ideas for setting the climate for inviting involvement and for keeping parents involved:

- Friendly smiles from the principal and staff should be shown to parents who pass by in the building.
- Remove fear and intimidation; also remove stereotypical attitudes that traditionally have been barriers. For example, "I'm the boss— you are just a parent!"
- Post a visitors' welcome sign at the front door or front hall. This expresses an invitation without anyone's being present to extend an open invitation.
- Make available a parents' room so they can conveniently meet with other parents.
- Provide a workroom equipped with toys and books for preschoolers.

- A monthly parents' luncheon helps to relax parents, and communication flows more freely from them.
- "Doughnuts for Dad" lets dads understand their importance in a special meeting just for them.
- Principals should encourage and set the tone for parents' involvement in the school.
- Teachers should be taught effective principles on how to best use parents' talents and make them partners.
- Tear down any invisible or visible walls indicating "you can't touch this." Often, parents are made to feel they are inferior to educators.
- Body language has proven to be a common barrier. Parents notice when administrators, teachers, and parent-leaders have not looked them in the eye when speaking. Other intimidating actions by administrators include wearing a blue suit every day, which shows authority, and certain facial expressions, gestures, and postures.

Involving Students to Reach Parents

When students are involved in positive ways, they become motivated, interested, excited, and challenged. They welcome more involvement and will even advertise programs to other students, to the community, to educators, and to parents.

Students Must Be Sold

The guidance counselor at an inner-city school sometimes seeks out the quiet students who seem to be unmotivated—students who don't fit in, as well as those who are unpopular or have some type of behavioral problem. This counselor has really tried to involve all students, knowing that the ones who are sold on school programs will then help their parents get involved.

It is well-known that when parents are involved, students are more successful. In this particular case, the students are fifth-through eighth-grade middle school adolescents who do not normally want their parents involved. Their parents, on the other hand, are eager to be invited to activities such as Honor Day and Parents Day to help them understand what is taking place at school. To encourage students, the guidance counselor created a school project so that students could come from each homeroom to work on it. They could add anything creative and constructive that might make them feel included and willing to go the extra mile—advertising ideas, artwork, decorations, announcements.

But this counselor was still challenged because none of the students wanted their parents involved. They didn't want to take home invitations to parents. So I went into each eighth-grade home-room to talk with students. I told them why I had been hired. Many of the students had seen me on television the previous night discussing my position as a parent-consultant. At this point, it became easier to get through to them. Most students were willing to participate once they understood they were the ones who would plan Parents Day. They were assured that there would be no negative talk from teachers to the parents—no one would "tell on them." This was going to be a fun time for their parents to come into the classroom to see what is going on.

Rewarding Participation

When Parents Day finally arrived, the eighth graders were very well-informed. The students received incentives for taking special invitations home and returning them to the school. Community and business resources were contacted as well. Guest speakers were planned and door prizes offered. Cakes were donated, and a hospitality room was set up where refreshments were served. The event was a great success.

As additional motivation for both students and parents, certificates were given out for student and parent participation. The result was that 60 of 300 parents came at different times from 9 a.m. to 5 p.m. Many parents said they wished they would be invited to school more often—they would find the time to visit. They also stated that it had been a long time since they had been students; this project had served as a good reminder of what it was like to be in school all day. It was a very positive experience.

Working With the Principal

One principal actively sets the atmosphere for parents at an inner-city elementary school. She grew up in a rural area and attended a one-room schoolhouse. This childhood experience has never left her heart, soul, or mind. Remembering her roots, she communicates her mission vividly and memorably to parents and staff with this motto: "Never give up on a child or a family."

This principal had to deal with a child who had previously attended many other schools in the system. She had developed a behavioral problem, and the principal felt that this was the child's last chance. She started to have problems again, so the principal called in the parent. When the mother did not show up, the principal called again, this time saying, "You cannot give up on this child. She's too important. Together, we can find the answers. I do not know what the answers are, but as we work together, we will make it together."

The mother said that this was the first time anyone in the field of education had ever expressed such words to her. She had lost faith in the school system. The mother and child were able to receive counseling from a local mental health association, which subsequently formed a school-based partnership on-site at the school.

When reaching out to parents, the principal also meets with teams consisting of parents and teachers who gather to freely offer suggestions for the school's improvement plan. In addition, those who volunteer at school are kept informed of activities via a parent mailbox. In her job, the principal is faced daily with "tough little customers," but she celebrates and praises parents when they stick by her in making plans for their children. She communicates her sense of gratitude by sending thank-you cards. As a principal in a Chapter 1 school with all types of social and economic challenges, she sets standards for others who want a safe, open climate with parents. Here are some of her suggestions to school leaders:

- Parents should feel *sincerity* and know that the principal, teachers, and staff genuinely care about them.
- Principals, staff, and parents should realize that they cannot reach their goals without a spirit of cooperation.
- Principals must spend time developing relationships with parents.
- Principals and teachers must be willing to admit to parents that they, too, make mistakes, that they do not know everything and cannot be and do everything for each child.
- A spirit of humor is absolutely essential to this enterprise—it breaks the ice.

The Need to Reach Out to Parents

Some parents come to their neighborhood school wearing hair rollers and house shoes. Many of them live right across the street and are at school every day because they see it as a safe environment.

Others live at a considerable distance from school, and although they would be dedicated parent volunteers, they have never been asked. No one has thought to include them, for example, in some service they could do from their homes.

This was the case with the parent of a youngster who was being bused to the other side of town. The parent was invited to school to discuss a problem her child was having. When the mother didn't come, the teacher thought she was uncaring. This same parent, however, was a good volunteer when her child attended a school near home, daily providing her services at school and checking up on her child. Sometimes, what we perceive as an "uncaring" attitude is actually a barrier in communication or a fear of the unknown.

Ensuring Safety

One of the seven characteristics of effective schools identified by researchers Ronald Edmonds and Lawrence Lezotte (see Lezotte & Jacoby, 1990, pp. 84-87) is a safe and orderly environment. In an effective school, there is "an orderly, purposeful businesslike atmosphere which is free from threat of physical harm. The school climate is not oppressive, and is conducive to teaching and learning" (Lezotte & Jacoby, 1990, p. 147).

In this context, the word *safe* represents a physical safety within the school building and its surroundings. An orderly, purposeful atmosphere is important for parent involvement as well as for children's learning. Parents should feel a sense of safety and security in the school building and surroundings. If they don't, they may not express their discomfort or fear; they simply will not attend meetings. Here are some ways your organization, along with school administrators, can create a sense of physical safety:

- All school safety and security policies should be set by members of a Plan to Action Committee. Create uniform rules throughout the district. For example, all schools can expel a student for bringing a gun to school. Be sure to include all stakeholders—students, parents, staff, educators, and community representatives.

- Get to know the residents in your area and invite them to visit the school. Form partnerships in school safety with them, such as a Join Hands in Safety program.
- Hold a safety development in-service for parents, educators, students, and community persons to help them understand the school safety mission.
- Practice a safety drill program at school.
- Instruct educators, parents, and students about how to talk to the media. Help parents solve problems by keeping in touch with other parents—a safety network. Ask administrators to hold press conferences to inform the public of the happenings at your school.
- Establish a "rumor" hotline for handling any controversy concerning the school. One local school director has a "concerns" hotline so that parents can record their questions on an answering machine. A coordinator then assists the director by returning the calls.
- Emotional trauma is real after any stressful situation. Professionals often focus only on students; however, from my experience, one cannot help the child until the family has been helped. When parents seem to be more traumatized than the students, they need the skills a professional can give in order to assist their child.

To ensure parent safety, one inner-city middle school holds its PTO meetings on Sunday afternoons, which increases parent involvement—most parents are not working. They are also less fearful of leaving their homes. In most areas, the crime rate is usually the lowest on Sundays.

Schools in a poverty-stricken crime area can hold evening meetings if buses are provided for parents and children and if policemen are placed inside and outside the meeting room. A school that tried this approach had meetings with standing room only. Even with the high rate of violence in the surrounding neighborhood, parents were supportive of their children's school.

Developing a Mission

Every organization, small or large, needs a clear, direct mission according to Stephen Covey (1989) in his book *The Seven Habits of Highly Effective People.* True success comes only after goals have been set by a planning committee or decision-making team. A mission statement puts these goals in concise written form, shows how they are related, and makes them available to remind team members and volunteers what their work is supposed to accomplish.

In *Principle-Centered Leadership,* Covey (1992) states that many executives do not understand what is involved in developing a mission statement. "It takes patience, a long-term perspective, and meaningful involvement" (p. 165). Frequently, there is a lack of commitment on the job, he says, because not everyone is involved. There needs to be a shared vision and values, the group must work together and implement the focus of the mission.

So often, parents and students at the secondary level are not involved in the visionary process. To make a good school, they should be included in all decisions. Administrators and their working partners are best served when they communicate information related to the family or school mission to all parties involved.

Empowering Parents

The *New Webster's Dictionary* (Bolander & Stodden, 1986) defines *empowerment* as "the giving of power." Synonyms for the word *power* include *ability, capability,* and *skill.* This section addresses the question, How does empowerment increase the partnership connection in education? By encouraging parents-partners to share in decision-making and management processes, educators can create a feeling of empowerment. Educators, please encourage parents to come up with answers on their own.

Building Confidence

When our Parent/Teacher Club was faced with opposition from teachers about too many parents in the building, the principal defended the parents' rights to be visible and involved. She asked the staff to find ways to involve them. Another principal said to his teachers, "If you do not want your high school students' parents here, you may get a transfer for the next school year." When actions like these are taken by the administrator, a "comfort zone" is provided for the parents. Parents feel welcome and safe; thus the partnership grows. Furthermore, positive relations develop between the staff, students, and entire families.

Parents at my child's inner-city school when I was president of the Parent/Teacher Club not only assumed new leadership, but many also decided to improve their skills or further their education. Some received their GEDs (general education diplomas) or took a more active role in their children's education. Parents returned to the workforce, even if it was only at a fast-food restaurant. I, for one, was inspired by the principal's vision to share the message that parents are lifesavers. I was amazed by the confidence she had in our parent group. We felt honored to be a part of the connection and to work closely with her! She taught and molded the parents, teachers, and students. Everything about her said, "I believe in you!"

For many years, parents have been called on only to participate in fund-raising projects or to do busywork when teachers do not have the time. These things are necessary, and it is beneficial to have somebody willing to do them. Too often, however, parents are not asked to participate in other aspects of the school's operation, such as classroom management, input about the curriculum, and disciplinary alternatives.

Traditionally, parents have been asked to discuss their professions, share video or photography skills, improve the lunch program, paint and decorate the cafeteria, and so forth. Nevertheless, more significant contributions can be made by parents to their child's school. Specifically, parents have valuable contributions to make in setting up goals for the school and in helping work out procedures for dealing with situations that arise on a day-to-day basis. A higher level of commitment and involvement will come from parents who are allowed to make policy decisions affecting their child's educational development.

According to one principal, "Empowerment does not mean a parent-partner taking over the running of the school . . . but to help and share in the policy-making process at the local school level, as well as at the district level." Children are not the only ones to benefit from this involvement. Parents' self-worth and self-esteem can rise dramatically, and teachers will receive much needed extra help and support.

In his book *Ready to Learn,* Dr. Ernest L. Boyer (1991), president of the Carnegie Foundation for the Advancement of Teaching, discusses the subject of empowered parents. "We recommend that pre-school PTAs be organized to give support to parents and build a bridge between home and school" (p. 33). This is true for all levels of education and for what partnerships are really about—building bridges.

Blending Diverse Interests

Concepts of blending were taught by the principal of the school where I volunteered. She said, "Always include *all* parents from *all* racial groups on committees." Perhaps minority parents feel they are not allowed a voice or have nothing to offer. But when their participation is sought and appreciated, they gain a positive sense of ownership about taking part in the education of their children. Minority parents are not just of color—a minority is any group smaller than the majority. Minorities may be educated or not, fat or skinny, low or high in socioeconomic status, and so on. If your school is located in an area where most parents have a high level of education, the parents who are not highly educated are members of a minority.

This school practiced multiculturalism and education in unity before we knew it had a name. The school and its parents were strengthened and empowered by the diversity of the learning community. Thus the entire school community was enriched.

Opportunities for Unity in Diversity

Opportunities to experience and learn about the diversified human population occurred daily at my children's inner-city school. An Australian singer came to perform, putting on two free concerts for the parents, teachers, and students. This was the first time many of the children had been exposed to another culture. We celebrated cultural differences and learned from each other—another form of blending. As you blend something into a mixture, it all becomes a part of a whole. This concept is included in the partners' group mission—to become one for the children.

In a Celebration of Unity, sponsored by our local district and presented by the Parents Are Lifesavers program, several schools participated that have English as a Second Language (ESL) programs. A potluck dinner featured food from all of the cultures represented, and families wore their native dress. Fliers were sent home in the native languages of the parents. To gain the support of bilingual-bicultural liaisons, personal invitations were extended at churches in the area that minister to people of different nationalities. Customary decorations of various countries added a festive touch to the evening. After dinner, districtwide ESL students performed native dances and songs. Workshops were used to explore the cultural history of the countries represented.

The festivities created harmony and unity as all cultural boundaries were removed. Joy was evidenced by the bonding of families, which might not have happened had it not been for this event. The information that participants had to offer about themselves helped the attendees to be more aware of the different cultures. Best of all, people were seen as individuals as we celebrated diversity.

It is important that community involvement not be confined to the school environment. An effort must also be made from within the community itself to develop trust and understanding by families. In addition, when putting together parent groups, be sure to blend parents who may live outside neighborhoods that are close to the school. One parent-teacher group holds it meetings in a church in the neighborhood where children live. This makes it easier for the parents who live far away to meet the teachers.

Overcoming the Challenges of Diversity

For any partnership in the school to work, all partners must be blended into the organized parent group, regardless of race, creed, or socioeconomic status. If the school population is varied in ethnic origin, creative steps should be taken to sensitively reach parents from the different cultural backgrounds. Some suggestions are listed next:

- Have principals and parent-leaders make sure that parents from all backgrounds have a representative on all of the school's committees.
- When dealing with non-English-speaking parents, it is imperative that significant time be allotted to allow parents to share their concerns. The atmosphere should be one of courtesy and sincerity.

Non-English-speaking families want respect—not just acceptance of their cultures. Because many parents are striving to overcome language barriers, allow them the freedom to express themselves freely without being interrupted.

- Parents who are not fluent in the English language have significant problems when volunteering with the school. Educators and parent-leaders should be sensitive about how they approach parents to volunteer. At the same time, they can feel confident that non-English-speaking parents are usually excited to share their stories, customs, and languages in teaching children.

- Parents who are not fluent in English may be used in a "telephone tree" using native languages. This does not take a lot of the parent's time and often gives them tremendous satisfaction.

- Parents who speak certain languages may be asked to translate materials from English to their languages.

- Some children have not heard another language spoken. Bilingual parents may read aloud to children in languages other than English.

- Parents not fluent in English must have workshops designed for their needs. This requires extra time, but it is necessary to meet the individual needs of this diverse population.

- Each principal who administers a large, diverse, non-English-speaking population should designate a committee whose primary objective is to support the parents' rights and responsibilities. This committee might consist of bilingual parents, educators, and community members. Someone (preferably bilingual) should be appointed to act as a liaison between the family and school. The advocate could bring any problems or concerns to the attention of the committee to decide how best to meet these challenges.

- Every school should provide resources such as

    - An ESL class for families at either the school or district level
    - Books translated into the native languages of students and families
    - Information about the development and care of children
    - A list of helping professionals in the area
    - Orientation to various governmental programs

Many parents are waiting and hoping for a chance to be part of a *team effort.* So often, I have heard teachers say that parents don't care. Nevertheless, the parents I know *do* care about their children's education.

Communicating With Partners

Clear communication is the key to keeping things running effectively. People need to know what is going on, what other people are thinking, and how their own efforts will contribute to the success of the programs in which they are involved. Here are some guidelines for effective communication:

- A teacher or a parent organization president must take the time to listen and to share ideas with parent partners.
- Parents and role models must take the time to listen to educators.
- Parents may communicate with other parents by way of a telephone tree network. Usually, this guarantees quick results. Parents tend to be responsive to their own peers.
- When listening, educators and parent-leaders should avoid being defensive or judgmental. Most people want their ideas and concerns to be heard and taken seriously.
- Teachers should ask parents for assistance.

In *Leadership Is an Art*, Max DePree (1989) states that in "most vital organizations, there is a common bond of interdependence, mutual interests, interlocking contributors, and simple joy. Part of the art of leadership is to see that this common bond is maintained and strengthened" (p. 101). This can be done when communication is open and clear. "What is good communication? What does it accomplish? It is the prerequisite for teaching and learning. It is the way people bridge the gaps formed by a growing company" (p. 101).

The same is true for schools. DePree says,

> People can stay in touch, build trust and ask for help, monitor performance, and share their vision. Good communication is not just simply sending and receiving, nor is good communication simply a mechanical exchange of data. No matter how good the communication, if no one listens, all is lost. The best communication forces you to listen. (p. 102)

An excellent way to communicate with parents is through a monthly newsletter containing information about both parent and classroom activities. The newsletter might even be produced by parents, with contributions from students and school staff, to be distributed in the classrooms for students to take home.

One way of communicating is to use a "wish list." Teachers list whatever services and materials they need to facilitate learning in their classrooms or in the school as a whole. Many parents have shared with me that they do not receive enough direction in building communication between all the participants. Knowing what teachers need for their classrooms can help build communication between all partners in the business of educating children.

Outcomes of
Effective Parent Involvement

Another principal effectively uses all six missing links at her school. She understands parent involvement; she has voting power on the school PTO board and feels it is her role to be a model of high expectations for the parents on the board. She has respect for individual differences and is open to suggestions from parents. This principal states that she does not participate in gossip and always tries to maintain impartiality plus a positive attitude toward teachers, parents, and students. It is extremely important for her to sustain a friendly, professional demeanor, which is especially helpful in creating a safe, friendly school environment.

This model principal tries to focus on team effort by bringing the parents in as players. When asked about the school improvement plan (mentioned in Chapter 1), she was pleased to share that parent volunteers are involved in shared-leadership training in which they learn how to give input into planning and decision making. They also develop classroom-type assessments, effective communication skills, and a better learning environment. Furthermore, parents at this school have revised the parent handbook.

She stressed that as an educator, the principal must "be ready to forego preplanned activities and interact with parents instead. Parents are our customers, and we must be willing to go the extra mile to make them feel comfortable and welcome." In addition, teachers and staff must be made aware through avenues such as in-services, meetings, and handbook preparation that parents make vital contributions.

This principal knows that it is very challenging to put the concept of blending into action. She told me,

> You can't force people to accept each other. On the other hand, you *can* be a role model and encourage and teach the concept of multiculturalism in the school. I try to treat everyone alike.
>
> One of my minority children had problems behaving. I arranged to have the parent ride with the child on the 30-minute school bus trip to the school. Once there, I concentrated on letting her know how important it was for her to see how the school operated and how her child performed in the classroom. We agreed that she was there to observe only; the child was not to speak to her, and she was not to discuss anything with the teacher during the class. Her first morning at the school, she watched as the students hugged me and talked with me before they went to their classrooms. Later, she told me that she liked the way I related to *all* the children. This started a new relationship of trust between her and her child and between her and the school.

I heard something very important from this principal: "You must believe what you teach! Parents and students are always going to be watching."

Both parents and teachers have mentioned benefits resulting from effective parent involvement. Some examples are listed as follows:

- Parents become active voices in favor of change.
- A partnership is developed and trust is created.
- Parents can stop rumors by focusing on the good within the school.
- Parents see firsthand what is happening in the school or classroom.
- Parent involvement helps increase academic achievement.
- Better student discipline is an obvious result.
- Financial assistance increases.
- Happy parents ensure good public relations for the school.
- Parents seem more willing to share their skills, occupations, and knowledge.
- Parents volunteer and give their support to the school.
- Parents act as mentors and leaders in their communities and with students.
- Parents, as a team, can bring about physical improvements at school or make suggestions to the central office.

Encouraging Parents to Keep Hope Alive

Reaching out to parents is often a difficult task. Most obstacles, however, can be overcome successfully when administrators set the tone, encourage teachers, and support parents and community members in forming partnerships. Yes, it does mean going the extra mile and going beyond the job description to meet parents' needs. As the examples in this book have pointed out, the results are well worth the journey—for every tenfold of effort, a thousandfold will be returned.

It does not matter where parents live—whether in public housing projects, urban areas, or suburbia; in fact, some are homeless. But all parents have the need to belong and feel ownership in their child's school.

Parents who get involved in school matters see firsthand what teachers, principals, and students face daily. They are then willing to be active voices for change and to improve their own parenting skills. Sometimes, it takes these extra minds, voices, and hands to ensure the highest quality of learning and enhance the community of caring learners.

In a parent-teacher group, there are invisible and visible walls that stop communication and parent participation in the school. One must be aware of how parent-partners are treated because of appearances or a lack of education. For example, I worked with a parent who had very poor hygiene habits yet was one of the school's most valuable parents. Because the principal and parents chose to use her talents, she felt important and began to work to improve her appearance.

Every parent is a teacher. Likewise, every teacher has more to learn. Although each is valuable as an individual, together they can form dynamic working partnerships. We can all find new ways to assist the partnering of parents and teachers in the activities of the school.

Here's a thought to remember: "A hundred years from now, it will not matter what my bank account was, the sort of house I lived in, or the kind of clothes I wore. But the world may be different because I was important in the life of a child" (Kathy Davis).

3 Forming a Volunteer Network
Starting From Scratch

The first two chapters have discussed the importance of extending the invitation and setting a climate for parent participation. Organization is the next vital step toward an effective parent and teacher collaboration.

As we began forming a volunteer network at my child's school, we met many challenges. We had few effective tools or proper instructions. Because we were left to come up with ideas of our own, we called around in search of quick steps toward successful school organization to help us get started. Fortunately, we already had some idea of the direction we wanted to take and a principal with an innovative vision. We had in mind to make our Parent/Teacher Club a vehicle that could implement the principal's concept of making *all* parents partners in children's education. We started with the information available to us and a little parent networking.

The Importance of Involving Everyone

It is possible to achieve your goals if you recognize that the work cannot be done by just one person. You must also have a unity of purpose. You do not always have to agree, but you do need to hold to a commitment and a willingness to work together for success. Volunteers at Napier achieved positive results by first assessing the school's needs and then involving all stakeholders—educators, parents, and members of the community.

Our team had a strong desire to reach out to all parents. We sent home a package of information and a volunteer interest form. We greeted parents as they entered the building, extending an open invitation to participate. Because parents from the inner city usually bring their children to school early to eat breakfast, we also used this opportunity to enlist their help.

To overcome any barriers that might hinder an inner-city parent from becoming involved, we called our group a "club" rather than an association or an organization. We stressed that every parent is important—whether poor or rich; black, yellow, or white; non-English speaking or English speaking; employed or not—all have the same need to feel safe and included in the educational matters of their child.

Our mission was to support the school's goals and to create an environment that would be nurturing and uplifting to all. Partnerships were formed regardless of the amount of money parents had, what they owned, or where they lived. We focused on the theme "Educators, Parents, and Community Involvement—It Works! It Works! It Works!"

Those who had never assumed leadership positions came forward to help. Partners who volunteered were trained to assist teachers both in the classroom and with their assigned duties. Jobs were created for all parents. We kept them informed, communicating with them on a weekly basis. We let them know what was going on and how they could contribute.

It was truly a miracle to see parents from the inner city to suburbia begin to work hand in hand. It was beautiful to see the people of the so-called disadvantaged areas forming a community of learners and givers. Together, we have indeed become lifesavers for students. Our volunteer network works!

Understanding Inner-City School Families

Researchers have found that children are a product of their home surroundings. Families who live in the inner city, however, often face special problems when they want to take an active part in their children's education. The lack of money is a huge barrier to many families who may have the time but insufficient financial resources to enable them to participate. Perhaps they have no bus fare or lunch money on days when they would like to volunteer. They may feel ashamed because they live in poverty. Some parents are embarrassed because they don't have the means to feed their children adequately. Or they may live where a lack of privacy makes it hard for their children to study or get enough sleep.

Other parents live in fear because they are in abusive or violent situations. Spousal and child abuse and the abuse of alcohol or drugs in the home hinder their commitment to service. These parents, especially the mothers, are frequently withdrawn and have trouble opening up to an educator or parent-leader. For example, in her heart a mother may want to be a room mother, but the climate at home leaves her with reservations. Furthermore, this concern may not be expressed to an educator or parent-leader.

A Parent Overcomes Fear

One parent who did overcome her fears called me when I was the Parent/Teacher Club president. She had taken her two children to a motel for homeless people to seek refuge from an abusive husband. Although I barely knew this parent, she called because she had nowhere else to turn. She said her husband had been physically abusing her, and she knew he would try to harm her again. She wanted to get back to her family in another state.

I called the YWCA Shelter for Battered Women and asked them what could be done. Their personnel sent a taxi first to pick up the mother and then went to school to pick up her two children. The driver took them to the bus station, and the YWCA even provided the fare. I never saw or heard from this parent again, but I took comfort in knowing that she was able to get out of town safely. This is just one example of the stressful things many parents must deal with on a daily basis.

Parents, no matter where they live, have a lot going on in their lives. Life in the 1990s can be very complex, and parents are sometimes overwhelmed. They need to be encouraged and taught how to be involved. It is good to be sensitive and very careful when approaching them. Do not make assumptions that they don't realize what is important. I have heard both educators and parents complain, "Some parents just don't care anymore." At the same time, parents say they are weary of being labeled as uncaring. Many of them are in desperate need of help; some are barely surviving, emotionally and socially, just trying to get through their day-to-day routines.

Inner-city parents *will* volunteer—just ask! This has been my experience on both the local level and district level. Give an explanation of what is needed; show them how to do the task at hand. Perhaps only a few volunteers will come forward at first. This does not mean you or your programs have failed. Nor is it time to give up. It may simply indicate that you must find new ways to get them involved. Focus on those who show an interest and build up their talents and strengths.

Keep Reaching Out—Parents Are Worth It!

Many parents, myself included, have had bad experiences in school because of physical, mental, social, and emotional trauma suffered during childhood. It is not easy for them to return to a place that reminds them of so much pain. Although it was no fault of my mother's, I did not grow up in what is labeled a "functional" family environment. I did not have wonderful learning experiences when I attended grade school, partly because my learning style and strengths were undeveloped. I went on, however, to become a successful wife, mother, friend, Parent/Teacher Club president, and parent consultant for our district. I have also succeeded in getting parents involved on a district and local school level.

Keep reaching out to your parents! Look beyond their excuses. If a lack of child care for preschoolers is a barrier, make an effort to provide child care. Offer lunches to volunteers who come from a distance or who may need financial assistance. To meet the educational goals of children, your organization must be willing to address family and community needs first. Search for a special parent-volunteer to coordinate an outreach program and give this person support. As you create a "We need you!" climate, you will be surprised at the turnaround.

At Napier, we incorporated as many community resources as possible into the classroom. For instance, scores of missionaries from area churches came to volunteer. Several clubs and organizations, such as Rotary Club, Buddies of Nashville, Pencil Adoptee Partners, and Real World (African American male mentors) sent volunteers to tutor the students. Foster grandparent volunteers came daily to read and kindle positive relationships with disadvantaged and emotionally troubled students. Reach out to wherever parents are—churches, neighborhoods, clubs, social gatherings, and sports events. An effective program touches the heart of the community.

Removing Invisible and Visible Barriers

As a word of caution, do not dwell on the problems of parents so much that you lose your own focus or start blaming instead of being constructive. The best leaders establish an inviting climate of trust and hope conducive for parents to give of their hearts and abilities. The three lists that follow provide practical information for gaining parent participation. Study them carefully to chart a positive course toward understanding, willingness, and action.

1. What Parent-Leaders and Educators Can Do. When you heed the following guidelines, you are taking steps to remove any obstacles to parent involvement.

- Examine yourself to see if you really want parent involvement.
- Have a pleasant smile for all parents.
- Be accessible to parents.
- Be aware of demographic patterns. In today's fast-paced society, many families move on a regular basis, and in most districts new students are enrolled daily.
- When planning events for parents, "set the stage." For example, if you are having coffee and doughnuts with them, make sure you and the setting are ready. Use tablecloths and have trays for pastries. This preparation makes parents feel welcome.
- *Never* gossip about a parent to another teacher or parent.
- Look within yourself for improvement.
- Be willing to share decisions with all parents.
- Practice including *all* parents.

- Listen carefully to suggestions from parents (you don't have to agree).
- Take a *risk* and try to involve the uninvolved.
- Recognize golden opportunities and use them with a sincere attitude.
- Write down your own personal goals; walk them, live by them. As Barth (1990) points out, you will "unlock" not only your own energy but also enable parents and students to empower themselves.

2. What Parents Say. The following list is based on interviews with parents and reveals what they believe are barriers to becoming involved at school:

- Parents feel that the principal is the key to removing barriers to parental involvement.
- Some feel that principals often fail to exercise the fair leadership necessary for positive partnerships.
- The principal and staff sometimes lack commitment to accept parents as partners.
- Teachers are not always receptive to parents.
- Too many teachers want parent involvement but are not supportive when "we come to the school."
- There is too little communication with the school.
- Teachers are afraid that parents will criticize; there is a lack of trust on the teachers' part.
- Parents fear they do not have enough education to be involved; they feel looked down on by the teachers.
- Frequently, parents feel they get only "lip service" from administrators, educators, and parent leaders.
- Parents feel negative attitudes and feelings from the school staff. Many times, they have been labeled as "those parents."
- Administrators, teachers, and parent-leaders are afraid of difficult or hard-to-manage volunteers, so they might avoid bringing in new people.

3. What Teachers Say. This information has been collected from teacher in-services that I have conducted. Teachers have listed what they see as barriers to parental involvement in their schools:

- Some teachers do not want parental involvement.
- There is no time for communication with parents.

- There are too many administrative duties: paperwork, filing, and so on.
- Often, single working parents are not given time to come to the school.
- A few parents are taking some form of drugs.
- Some parents reside in a distant neighborhood.
- Parents do not seem to care about their children.
- Parents are not supportive of class instruction.
- Parents lack the education needed to help their children.
- Parents want to control the curriculum, teaching program, and so on.
- Time is a major barrier. For example, because they teach all day and are without convenient access to a telephone, many teachers find it difficult to reach parents. It is not uncommon for a student to list his or her residential number in August only to have the teacher call in November and find the number invalid.
- Some parent volunteers do not get along with principals, parents, or teachers.
- Some parents are disruptive in the classroom and are abusive to other parents and to students.
- Parents sometimes fear the differences of race, gender, and background of the administrator, teachers, and other parents.
- Some parents are homeless, have no transportation or telephone, are poor, have poor hygiene habits, and are uneducated.
- When the administration gives lip service, at either the district or local level, this creates barriers to parental involvement.

Once educators have been taught during an in-service how to nurture meaningful parent partnerships, attitudes begin to change. Most educators sincerely want successful parent involvement, but they lack proper tools and instructions. A volunteer network helps remove the obstacles just mentioned, benefiting all team players who influence a child's education.

Before Getting Organized

Before organizing a volunteer network, it is important to find out what regulations exist that will affect the way you go about structuring and running your group. Many states have laws mandating parent organizations, associations, or both that are quite specific regarding what can and cannot be done. Call your superintendent's office to find out more about specific regulations concerning your district or state PTA councils.

Study Education Reform Mandates

Among the many recent education reform mandates across the country is that of the New York State Decentralization Law. Some of the New York law requirements are given here as a guide to your planning.

The law requires all public schools in the state to have either a parent association or a parent-teacher association. When a school has neither, the principal is responsible for encouraging parents to organize such an association.

It is the participants' choice whether or not to organize an association of parents that includes teachers. The bylaws are to be written by the parents, and an annual election must be held to elect officers. The administrative personnel, principal, community superintendents, high school superintendents, and the executive director of special education have no right to interfere with the internal affairs of this association.

Organizations in New York schools may have as many fundraising events as needed, but only two activities a year involving children during school hours are permitted. The association may not sell tickets for children to attend movies or theaters unless the activity is directly connected with the curriculum. The law further states that children may not sell raffle tickets or be involved in any other form of gambling. On the other hand, children may distribute flyers, bulletins, and letters to parents, if the information contained is suitable for such distribution by children.

If your state does not have laws or regulations regarding parent involvement, the school board or school superintendent's office in your district should. If you do not familiarize yourself with these mandates, you may find yourself planning an activity that is not allowed by regulations. Furthermore, you may never find out about helpful regulations that suggest ideas of value to your organization.

Choose the Type of Organization

I interviewed several principals to see what types of organizations are available. Not every school has an official association that all parents can join. I discovered, nevertheless, four basic types of organizations that are active in schools.

1. A **PTA** (parent-teacher association) is connected with the state and national association. When membership dues are paid by parents to a local school PTA, a small portion of the total is allotted to the state, with a percentage also going to the national office. Many middle and high school associations include students who belong to PTSAs (parent-teacher-student associations). PTSAs offer a special forum in which students are invited to give their input in discussions.

2. A **PTO** (parent-teacher organization) is an organization with an independent nature. Dues are collected, all of which are designated for use in that school. The PTO is not affiliated with a state or national organization. Students in middle and high schools are also encouraged to join, forming a PTSO (parent-teacher-student organization).

3. A **PTC** (parent-teacher club) is used in schools where it is important to help parents feel less threatened about being involved.

4. An **SAC** (school advisory committee), SSC (school site council), or SBD (site-based decision-making team) is made up of groups of students, parents, community leaders, and educators who serve as representatives of the larger population. A kind of committee is usually set up to share information and to help make major decisions regarding school policy and activities.

Creating a Plan to Action

Once you have found out what regulations may affect your organization and decided what form your group should take, it is time to develop a plan to action to help your organization design a method for achieving its goals.

An effective volunteer program is vital to the success of any school. Getting such a program launched and enlisting volunteers to help, both on and off school premises, should be the major goal for your organization. School volunteers can help in a multitude of areas: student learning, truancy, gangs, safety, increasing school spirit, heightening student self-esteem, breaking cultural barriers, and so on. Without the assistance provided by dedicated parent and community volunteers, most schools would be unable to offer many of the extra learning experiences that students deserve.

Sample Plan to Action

The following plan to action includes a calendar of events used by some schools in building a volunteer network. Your organization may wish to make alterations to suit specific needs.

May—Form the Plan to Action Steering Committee for the upcoming school year. Begin now to form a committee that will meet in July. An advisory or steering committee should consist of diverse key persons—the principal, one or more teachers, community leaders, and interested parents plus designated representatives of the PTA or PTO, if one already exists. They will assess the needs of the school and the new organization.

If a PTA or PTO does not exist, mail home a general invitation asking if parents would be willing to participate. Your PTA or PTO may want to merge with the Plan to Action Steering Committee. Because some organizations do not have strong leadership, this is necessary. In any case, the PTA or PTO president should be a facilitator for the committee. Remember to include non-English-speaking parents or community leaders if they are part of your constituency. Also, try to make arrangements ahead of time for parents who lack transportation or work during the week. Finally, plan a calendar of activities for the August-to-July school year.

July—Create job descriptions of committee members and others at the Plan to Action Steering Committee meeting. If a set of working bylaws does not already exist, the steering committee (or a separate committee) will formulate a detailed written description of functions, upcoming budgets, duties, and responsibilities of each officer and committee chairperson in your organization. To do this, assess the school's needs and what is being done or what can be done. Come up with ideas about how to support the school in its primary objective of educating all students. Remember, needs may vary, so make your list without relying too much on ideas from other schools or lists you may find in this book.

At this time, negotiate the limits or guidelines for parent participation. Will parents be allowed to participate in decision making, such as school discipline, budget, curriculum, hiring, and so on? From the beginning, there should be a clear understanding communicated in writing about what is "off limits" to parents. These should be *mutual* decisions between the school staff and the parents, not mandates unilaterally imposed by the principal. Be aware that state law or district employee contracts may restrict what parents are permitted to do at site-based levels.

Put together a packet of information for parents. Include a membership letter asking parents and teachers to join the parent-teacher group (see sample in the Resources section of this book). Inform people how the dues will be used. In the packet, provide a return printed envelope (name, amount, homeroom) for the membership dues, a family volunteer interest form, and a calendar of events. Because there will be a lot of printing involved, you may wish to negotiate a discount at a nearby print shop. Perhaps you may get the printing free as a donation to the school. Remember to supply your tax number to avoid paying any unnecessary costs.

August—Conduct a tour of the school for students and parents before the first day of the new school year. One way to bridge the gap between parents and the school is to provide an orientation tour of the school before the new school year. At this time, faculty and staff members can be introduced, thereby allowing parents to feel a sense of ownership and belonging.

It is also a good time to begin a public relations campaign. A few parents can be selected as leaders to let the community know what's going on at the school. Be sure to design a welcoming exhibit to help parents feel at home when they enter the school building. Everyone knows the lasting impact of a first impression.

August—Deliver the previously prepared parent-teacher information packets to parents. The information generated by the committee can be given out at the school tour (or sent home for those who do not attend). In addition, the principal should extend a verbal invitation to the parents describing various ways their expertise can be used by the school. Most PTAs and PTOs allow a period of time, such as one month, to enroll parents and teachers in their organization.

September—Send out public relations letters to request volunteers and announce events. Letters can be sent to the following organizations and individuals in the community, requesting volunteers: churches, the media, Retired Senior Volunteer Programs (RSVP), the Chamber of Commerce (to inform businesses and parents' employers), sororities and fraternities, the Jewish Federation, the National Association for the Advancement of Colored People (NAACP), Junior League, United Way, elected city and state officials, the Rotary Club, Adopt-a-School Foundation, Junior Achievement, the YMCA and YWCA, and local community colleges and universities.

Before every event, distribute a press release stating all the pertinent information—who, what, when, and where. Send out a mailing 2 weeks before events are to take place. Follow up with phone calls. Be sure to take advantage of public service announcements and community announcements by sending complete information to radio, newspaper, and television personnel. With all the support generated by media partners, your volunteer network will be a success. It will work!

September—Hold an orientation for volunteers. In the first few weeks of the new school year, call together parent volunteers who have returned the volunteer enlistment forms (see sample in the Resources section of this book) included in the information packet. This is the time to clearly define school policies regarding volunteers. If your school or district has a volunteer handbook, use it and provide copies; if no handbook exists, create one. The National School Volunteer Program distributes *Volunteers and Older Students,* a publication to help you start or improve your program (see the Resources section of this book). Volunteers should have training in leadership advocacy and in chairing and conducting special programs within the school.

The orientation should include a presentation of policies, regulations, and rules. The following are examples of what parents need to know:

- The fact that parents may not administer corporal punishment to any students

- Where to get a health test or tuberculin skin test, if required
- Procedures for using the copier, overhead projectors, and other school equipment, including a hands-on introduction
- A warning that parents should not come to school on days when they have a bad cough, cold, fever, or sore throat
- A written description for each parent in his or her native language of the job he or she will be asked to do (see the sample job description in the Resources section of this book)

This last point is extremely important. Communicate clearly from the beginning what duties are to be performed and when they must be completed. If volunteers do not follow through with assignments, it is usually because they do not understand the directions or the time limits. Volunteer partners should be allowed to say no. Maybe the timing is not right for their participation now, but there will be another opportunity for them in the future.

October—Host the first official Open House meeting. An Open House can serve several purposes aside from getting parents into the school. It can foster enthusiasm, encourage parental support, and heighten educational awareness. Begin by having steering committee members call from their homes to invite parents and their relatives. Provide callers with rosters of all parents they are to contact.

Create a warm, friendly climate at your Open House by allowing volunteers to welcome parents and serve refreshments. Volunteers can also collect membership dues, sell T-shirts, and keep a few people from being overburdened. This gives other parents an opportunity to socialize or meet their child's teacher.

The Open House program should introduce officers and recognize parents and community members who have volunteered to be part of the parent-teacher group. This is a good time to hear suggestions for creative fund-raising as well. You will need at least one or two persons to chair fund-raiser events, so look for trustworthy individuals who are competent in money management.

October—The Plan to Action Steering Committee meets with homeroom parents. Ideally, this meeting is held in early October to plan for fall events and school celebrations. It is a good time to say thank you to supporters and prepare for American education events that occur in

November across the nation. It is also a good time to compile a teachers' wish list.

November—Ask interested parents, the principal, and teachers to join the Plan to Action Steering Committee meeting at the end of November to discuss upcoming winter activities. You may want to plan a sharing time before school opens and serve breakfast or brunch.

December—Schedule a multicultural "Holiday Happening" as your PTA or PTO meeting. The hospitality and refreshment coordinators will oversee this special time. It is an excellent occasion for blending diverse families and having them share their values as well as learn about customs from around the world. The program will show respect and appreciation for each family's differences. During a multicultural Holiday Happening, cultural differences are high-lighted. Parents are asked to bring artifacts and foods commonly prepared in their native lands. The PTA or PTO plans a special program to honor all types of families and traditions. For example, December 13 is Saint Lucia Day, a Swedish holiday. Girls might dress in white gowns and wear crowns on their heads.

January—Kick off "Winterfest" workshops. The PTA or PTO will host a Winterfest, funded by the PTA or PTO budget and a teachers' minigrant. Family, school, and community partnerships offer grants to teachers who wish to build bridges between teachers and parents as partners. Invite families to attend. A series of workshops will feature topics such as how to involve children in making winter artwork and how to have better family relationships.

January—Meet to prepare for the rest of the school year. Describe up-coming events, such as a teachers' appreciation luncheon, April fund-raisers, a volunteer appreciation brunch, and so on. Enlist volunteers to sign up after the meeting and ask for input from parents and teachers. Have a suggestion box near the front door along with paper and pens.

February—Hold a second set of workshops for parents. Choose interest-ing topics, such as how to create a heart connection with our children or teaching with more than an attitude of tolerance.

It is time to get ready for another PTA or PTO meeting, perhaps with the theme "Brotherhood-Sisterhood Week." Students could put on a program about getting along even with our deepest differences.

March—Formalize plans for a teachers' appreciation luncheon. Two parents should be recruited from each homeroom to organize parents in hosting a luncheon for teachers. Each classroom will be asked to bring several dishes, and the PTA or PTO will provide paper goods, gifts, decorations, and drinks.

Spring Break! Yes!

April—Plan for the new school year. Plan a spring fund-raiser so that your PTA or PTO will have money to start fresh after all bills have been paid from the previous school year. Plan an audit so the books can be cleared out in May.

May—Plan a volunteer appreciation event with the principal and staff. All volunteers who have helped touch the lives of children at school should be invited. Ask each teacher and staff member to contribute several items to the brunch.

The Plan to Action Steering Committee should also meet with the new PTA or PTO officers to discuss a change of committee members for the upcoming year.

More Ideas for a Successful Network

Although most educational partners do not have a lot of money to give, they have countless hours, talents, and abilities that they are willing to share. Remember that not everything done *for* the school has to be done *at* the school. Many valuable contributions are made from volunteers' homes or offices. In addition, make giving awards an ongoing aspect of the volunteer program. Thank-you notes should be sent to businesses that allow employees to tutor on release time.

All too often, the school misses critical opportunities because some parents are left out. Perhaps certain positions have been held too long by the same persons or groups. It is easy for parents to feel that a particular clique is being favored and that their services are not welcome. Everyone willing to help should be given a chance to do something. A volunteer position, starting with the president on down, should be rotated yearly. If a parent fills out a participation form expressing a willingness and a desire to help, the offer needs to be accepted in a timely way. Early in the year, organize jobs into categories and know who is available for what service. Also let parents know when they will likely be called on to do a job.

Volunteers who act as mentors, tutors, or foster grandparents should be evaluated regularly to ensure that goals are being met. For example, if someone is to give a child extra attention by reading to him or her, this objective needs to be followed through on.

Volunteers are such an inherent part of the school that they need to be informed where and when events are to occur. A copy of the newsletter should also be sent to them as well as to local newspapers, churches, elected officials, administrative bodies, and members of the school board.

In summary, attention to organization is the key ingredient to keep in mind when trying to successfully involve a diverse group of parents, educators, and community stakeholders.

4 Using Parents' Expertise

It is important to identify and *fully* use the particular skills and interests of parents in the schools. There is still a lack of knowledge and considerable resistance concerning parent involvement, even after 25 years of research. Nevertheless, many districts are trying to build bridges between schools and parents, and leaders are putting the theory and results of research into practice.

Five Avenues for Parent Participation

Dr. Joyce L. Epstein is a principal researcher at the Center on Families, Communities, Schools, and Children's Learning in Baltimore, Maryland. In her article "Making Parents Your Partners" (Epstein, 1993), she identifies five types of parental involvement:

1. Parenting—The school helps parents create a supportive learning environment at home.
2. Communication—The school reaches parents through effective communication.
3. Volunteering—The school recruits and organizes parent help.
4. Learning at home—The school provides parents with ideas for helping children at home.
5. Representing other parents—The school recruits and trains parent-leaders. (p. 52)

Parents Are Already Involved

One way of thinking about parents is to recognize that they are already involved in education. Parenting begins at conception, for better or worse. It is a demanding and complex job that is directly related to the self-esteem of the caretakers. When they discover that becoming involved at school makes them feel good about themselves and their families, they want to get even more involved. It is the school's responsibility to help parents embark on this effort.

On the whole, parents are trying to understand the learning process of their children. This is usually accomplished through weekly or monthly newsletters, report cards, and progress reports from the school. Parents are required to sign reports and return them—a form of communication and involvement on the parents' part.

Parents are also involved when they sit with their children at the kitchen table doing homework—often for 2 hours or more every day. Some parents do even more and visit the school, volunteer, or become a parent-leader.

In 1993, our district allowed us to have Parent Appreciation Day during American Education Week. We sent out invitations to parents throughout the district and invited the former state commissioner of education as well as our state senator. The children sang, and we served refreshments and awarded door prizes. This was our opportunity to let parents know that they are lifesavers. Many parents later commented about how grateful they were to be recognized as an instrument in their child's education.

The Qualities of Leadership

Every parent-teacher organization, whether an advisory board or a participant group, depends on the quality of its leadership. A leader must realize the potential for the group. In his book *Communicate,* Verderber (1975) defines *leadership* as "exerting influence to bring about changes in attitudes or actions of others" (p. 138). Max DePree (1989) states in *Leadership Is an Art* that leaders must also be servants. Too often, parent groups do not realize that they must set an example; they must not seek glory for themselves as individuals or even as a group. Servant leaders try to work in a united effort to build a community of caring adults. They must be committed, willing to take a stand, and able to make a decision and hold to it if they feel it is right. They must also create cohesiveness and give worthy praise.

For the group to be effective, the leader must arrange for a meeting place, prepare and plan the agenda ahead of time, bring up topics and policies, and allow all who wish to voice their opinions to do so. He or she must ask questions whenever necessary and summarize the content of the meeting.

Three Types of Leadership Style

An *authoritarian* leader takes on a dictatorial responsibility toward policies and procedures. This type of leader can get a lot of paperwork done but may also end up hurting a lot of feelings. On the outside, it seems as if everyone is pulling together, but on the inside, there is nothing but chaos because no one will speak out. Because their opinions are not respected, authoritarian leaders lack followers. They rule with fear and intimidation, and most coworkers just do what they have to do, saying as little as possible. Have you ever been faced with a dictatorial leader?

The *democratic* leader is person oriented and works well sharing power with others. This leader may take ultimate responsibility for the actions of the group but only after giving all involved a chance to express themselves. He or she assures others that they have been carefully and respectfully heard. This leader makes suggestions and clarifications while supporting, listening, encouraging, and facilitating the whole group—without fear and intimidation. How do you feel when working with a democratic leader?

The *laissez-faire* leader provides no leadership at all. This person gives information only if asked, and no one is in charge. I have seen far too many laissez-faire leaders in parent groups—just spinning around, not knowing what to do.

Democratic Leadership Is Needed

Research supports my experience that a democratic style of leadership is necessary to have an effective parent-teacher group. Every parent-training program should encourage parents to act according to principles that seek to empower all parents and create a positive experience for everyone. The following list of principles will help prepare leaders and those who select people for leadership positions:

- Every parent and child is a potential leader.
- Those in leadership positions influence other people (this can be for the better or worse).
- We are all leaders in our lives, whether we want to be or not.
- The best leaders are facilitators who give parents the confidence to step forward. A president's job is not to rule but to identify parents' individual leadership strengths and build on them.
- Leaders' actions should reflect a sincere commitment to the objectives of the organization.
- Leaders set the example for the entire learning community. Parents will want to model their example. They should provide a climate of high expectation in a safe and orderly environment. If parents feel safe, they will come out to the school and take part in volunteering.
- You can do anything—but not everything. Leaders build on team effort, set priorities, develop short- and long-term goals at the beginning of each school year, and review progress at the end of each year.
- The leader needs assistance in carrying out organization goals. This can be achieved through delegation and involves four steps:
  - Evaluation of the organization—the leader must understand the ongoing evaluation needs of the parent-teacher group and the overall program. Be open for suggestions and to change.
  - Agreement—Tasks that parents are to do should be clearly explained, including what is expected, when it is expected, and how it is to be done. When you ask someone to do something, follow up with sufficient communication.
  - Support—The leader's influence can be extended in many ways. The leader can refrain from criticizing, ask parents what they might need, and send a thank-you note for jobs well done.
  - Follow-up—Parents should not be left to fend for themselves after agreeing to an assignment. Give them an opportunity to discuss their progress and to obtain help if needed.

- Remember the golden rule: "Do unto others as you would have them do unto you." Put yourself in the shoes of your volunteers and treat them with kindness.

What Can Volunteers Do?

There are many things parents can do as volunteers. Some things can be done at home, and others need to be done at the school. Parents should choose where they would like to be involved and the amount of time and energy they want to commit. A suggested time commitment is less than 2 hours a week.

Four Areas of Participation

There are four general areas of parent involvement in the schools. Most schoolwide projects will require support in one or more of the four areas: classroom participation, fund-raising, site-based decision making, and school-business-community relations. The parent participation ideas listed next are loosely organized into these four areas. Please note that some of the suggestions can apply to more than one category.

Classroom Participation

- Be a room parent or teacher's assistant.
- Phone other parents to inform them of what is going on.
- Attend day or night workshops to learn how to be a lifesaver in a child's education.
- Read to a child at school.
- Reinforce and supplement the academic endeavors of a child by becoming a tutor.
- Save supplies for math, science, art, or social studies (such as buttons, fabric, yarns, pop bottles, socks, rocks, and toothpicks).
- Sew curtains, chair covers, and so on—make things that may be needed in the school.
- Share your ideas with a classroom, including those about your work or hobbies.
- Grade papers.
- Prepare bulletin boards for teachers.
- Assist with artwork.
- Share a foreign language or discuss another country that you have visited.

Fund-Raising

- Write letters to request donations, apply for grants, or elect officials.
- Help organize or participate in (or both) a bake sale.
- Have a car wash as a fund-raiser.
- Participate in a general store fund-raiser (see p. 52).
- Provide supplies for special events or projects.
- Provide treats for career fairs, carnivals, teachers' appreciation days, and parties.
- Provide money for students who aren't able to afford field trips.

Site-Based Decision Making

- Stand up for students' rights in appropriate meetings and forums.
- Serve on a participatory management team, parent-teacher advisory board, or school improvement team.
- Serve on special committees, such as the bus safety committee.
- Promote school safety by walking the halls, monitoring the lunchroom, or supervising after-school games.
- Be a representative to an advisory organization, such as in the federally funded Chapter 1 L Pack program.
- Serve on the recycling committee.
- Represent other parents on the district board.

School-Business-Community Relations

- Inform the media of upcoming events.
- Help in the office.
- Give computer training.
- Type newsletters.
- Assist the school staff wherever needed.
- Act as host or hostess to guests visiting the school.
- Do yard work to keep the school grounds looking beautiful.

How to Include Parents:
Tricks of the Trade

Following are some well-tested ways to encourage parental and community involvement. Administrators, educators, and parent-leaders will want to build on this list to tap the valuable talents and services waiting to be shared by parents and the community. The ideas that follow, loosely organized according to the four areas of parent participation, can serve as a guideline for how to begin

Classroom Participation

Make a wish list of what is needed for the individual classrooms. Parents, friends, and relatives have the time and the resources to help teachers and staff if they are allowed to do so.

A letter-writing campaign instituted by the principal and PTO is a way to say, "We're here—we need your help!" Don't be surprised if someone responds with, "Come by and pick up $100 worth of school supplies—you have our support." This happens at Napier over and over again.

Often, churches in the area offer tutoring at the school or the church itself. A parent's church group may be willing to adopt a classroom. Be sure that this activity does not offend students and families of differing faiths.

Many universities offer education classes in which the students (mostly early childhood development and elementary education majors) are required to complete a community project. You can bring these students into your school to help. Describe your needs to a college teacher and see if the necessary arrangements can be made.

Many schools ask parents to pledge a certain amount of time to benefit the school. This commits parents to become partners in education.

Fund-Raising

Pass around a cash donation box at all of your meetings. This is how Napier bought its telephone answering machine.

At the end of spring, many schools have all kinds of fun days, field days, or carnivals. The money from such an event can be used to kick off the first day of the next school year.

Put on a benefit supper for the entire community to raise proceeds for the school. This brings people together and gives them an opportunity to share and to serve. Ask local restaurants to donate tableware and food items, contacting them well in advance of the event.

A small, child-oriented "general store" can be set up on the stage of your school auditorium each month from noon to 2 p.m. Children buy 25¢ tickets during the hour before school. They are allowed to purchase items donated by the parents, such as books, clothing, cupcakes, or toys. Send home a note before the event saying, "We need your help. Please send items for the general store; and please come and volunteer." We normally raise approximately $270 each time we have this event. This is a wonderful way of including parents and benefiting the school at the same time.

Site-Based Decision Making

Get parents to voice their concerns at school board meetings. Remember to be positive.

Learn to empower parents by creating jobs for them with the school. This tip is essential for having an effective PTO and for developing parent leadership.

The talents of extended family members can be used in many ways. Grandparents, for example, can make phone calls to latchkey children, give aid to classroom teachers, walk hallways, and give the benefit of their knowledge. Often, senior citizens are excellent role models. They can play a vital role in the educational process even if they don't have a relative in your school.

School-Business-Community Relations

Send out a letter requesting volunteers (see the sample in the Resources section of this book). Send letters to churches, sororities, fraternities, and private organizations. Let people know that your organization exists, that their help is needed, and that you would appreciate their assistance.

Free public service announcements will let others know what you need for your school—volunteers, supplies, or donations.

Work with the Big Brother/Big Sister programs to foster positive relationships between adult mentors in the community and children. Administrators can give permission for a big brother or sister to visit his or her little buddy at school. This is especially supportive to single-parent families.

Foster grandparent programs, often funded by United Way, bring positive male and female role models from the community into the schools. The seniors feel needed, and students receive the special wisdom and nurturing that only a grandparent can give.

Always show appreciation to parents, businesses, and community members by sending them thank-you notes for their time, goods, or money. Mention their names and business or service in the parent newsletter and host a volunteer luncheon in their honor.

School-Parent Relationships That Work

Parents of Special Education Children Pitch In

The principal of a special education school has 120 disabled students enrolled in his school, one fourth of whom live in institutions or reside in foster care. Parents of these students are often overburdened and do not understand the need to be involved.

When new PTA copresidents took leadership several years ago, they found only 10 people attending the meetings. The PTA team struggled with how to get more parent participation. I was invited to speak to them about developing a plan to action to involve more educators, parents, and community members. About 30 people attended a potluck dinner meeting, complete with door prizes. I spoke about the parent-teacher relationship, about how partnerships were instrumental in making the school a success.

Using a Phone Tree Network and Motivating Teachers

After that, they all began working on new, innovative ideas to increase school partnerships. A room parent was assigned to each of their 14 classrooms—this was their "phone tree network." Because many of these parents do not have their own transportation, the copresidents sent out a notice 1 week before and 3 days before every meeting, followed by a call to see if parents needed transportation.

One teacher said he was elated to finally see the parents of his students at a meeting.

Little by little, attendance increased at the potluck meetings. Families came with children in wheelchairs and on crutches; they came without disabled children as well. A guest speaker—someone who could relate to the needs of the special education family—was featured each time.

The teachers complained at first. "The parents don't come— why should we? It's a parent-teacher association, not a teacher association." At that point, the copresidents allotted teachers a $10 voucher for supplies if they had four people in attendance (counting the teacher, the assistant, and at least two parents). And if they went to every one of the meetings, they would get $40, which was designated to go toward an extra bus trip for the year. The incentives really got the teachers excited and motivated.

Benefiting From Fund-Raisers

The parents of this special school have gone above and beyond the call of duty. The following is an example of one of their innovative fund-raisers. When a football game was to be held across the street from the school, the principal had an idea—to park cars on the school grounds. The parents got together, provided a sitter for the children, and pulled together to make this project a great success. The school made about $2,000 from parking the cars.

At their auction fund-raiser, two parents raised $6,500, with only 125 people in attendance. Parents bought every item donated, including $450 worth of legal services and a vacation weekend, items these families were able to obtain at much less than market value. A parent also donated the hot dogs and chili refreshments! The school and parent-teacher group asked for donations from the community because they wanted to create a more unified environment. It worked!

To keep up enthusiasm before the auction, incoming donations were posted on a hallway bulletin board every day. Teachers saw the list grow from 6 to 20 to 50 items, then 80 items—then they really got excited. That's when they really began to want to take part.

An owner of a sign company donated a $3,000 marquis sign to the school on behalf of his son. This came about when the PTA president called the sign company to rent a sign for the auction. The company ended up building and giving the school the sign, free of charge. Now the school can advertise for anything it needs. Amazing things happen when parents put forth the effort and build on the strengths of parents.

The PTA auction chairperson told me that it had been a very difficult project because so few people were willing to help. Parents had good reasons for not participating, largely because they were under such great stress. But those who showed up were extremely committed and wanted the program to succeed. Even with their special needs, these parents still sacrificed time and energy to go to the school daily for 2 months to make the auction a success.

Eighth Graders' Parents Become Partners

Parents as Partners is a successful inner-city school program for eighth-grade students. The program was initiated a few years ago by an eighth-grade guidance counselor, the PTO president, two team teachers, and a bilingual teacher who recognized the importance of parental influence on student success.

First, the team got together and wrote a grant proposal, deciding what they were going to do, what items were needed, and what would be their focal point. They used creative ideas from teachers who wanted to do different kinds of hands-on activities with students. They all worked together to develop the goals of the project.

The next step was to delineate specific areas of parental participation. You might also try some of their ideas:

- Create a parent needs assessment form.
- Create a volunteer list.
- Get to know your parent-teacher group officers.
- Organize special parent groups.
- Create a parent counselor or parent-teacher newsletter.
- Conduct parent-teacher conferences.
- Plan special programs for parents.
- Organize parents to contact other parents.
- Send "happy notes" home regarding something positive a child has done.
- Invite parents to serve on guidance committees.

Parents Have Always Been Welcome

I visited an inner-city school that has 40% African American and 60% Caucasian children. Only 45% of the parents have a high school or college education. The principal told me that parents have been welcome here since his arrival in 1966—before school reform, school improvement plans, or mandates.

The principal said, "I have always supported parental involvement, and it has been a wonderful experience. Volunteers have eased the load for the administration, staff, and teachers. The benefits to children are getting better grades, being happier in school, and seeing their parents in the building." By the way, this school has enjoyed excellent public relations because of the high level of parental involvement.

Teachers begin each year in a faculty meeting, discussing how they plan to get parents involved. The principal and the PTA invite parents to a coffee to get acquainted. This school recently received 3,016 hours of volunteer service from 301 volunteers in one year. The PTA president stated that she has never been in the school when there were no parents on the premises.

When I asked about fund-raising, I learned from the PTA president that "it is very important because our schools cannot provide all that is needed for the children." All 23 classrooms have TVs and soon will have VCRs and computers. One positive aspect of fund-raising is that it creates opportunities for bonding between the parents.

Caught You Being Good

The PTA and faculty work with parents to give positive feedback to students. The Gold Slip Program has for its motto, "Caught you being good." Parents stand in the hallways, in the cafeteria, and on the playground. If the children are doing some wonderful thing, such as picking up trash, demonstrating good behavior in the lunchroom, or walking in an orderly way down the hallway, they are given a gold slip. At the end of the month, these students are rewarded by the principal in assembly. Besides increasing good discipline, this program helps parents to become involved.

I'm So Proud

"I'm So Proud" is a motivational program for rewarding the use of good manners. Children who are chosen are awarded a badge while eating lunch. Twice a month, these children eat lunch from McDonald's (purchased by the PTA) up on the stage with the principal.

Mentors for Students

A mentorship program is available at this school for children who are economically and culturally deprived. Many of them need an extra boost for their self-esteem. Sometimes, mentors read to the children or give them treats whenever they achieve good grades. This is not a tutoring project but a "feel-good-about-yourself" activity. I was told that the school never had a single teacher resist any parent participation project; the teachers have always considered the parents to be important. Perhaps this is a result of the principal setting the tone.

In summary, it is extremely necessary to use parents' expertise, skills, and particular interests in these times when budget cuts for schools are commonplace. To overcome any parent resistance, nudges help build teamwork and confidence in educators, parents, and students. Create a plan to action to come up with possible solutions to use parents in the schools. Get students at your particular school excited and involved in the overall process, too.

When I conduct a high school, middle school, or special education in-service, I see that the barriers and problems are the same. Educators are constantly asking me how they can get parents involved. We must problem solve together using innovative techniques. By being creative, taking the initiative, and involving parents and their talents in worthwhile ways, we will all benefit.

| Parents are lifesavers in children's education! |

5 Strategies for Successful Parent Involvement

Community-Based Foundation Grants

In Chapter 4, we explored a number of ways to use parents' expertise in the schools. Now that the partners are willing and ready to work together, they may be looking for a way to fund their vision.

A major focus of this chapter is to relate how a few principals in the Metropolitan Nashville Public School District have used funding from a public, nonprofit community foundation to encourage parent and community involvement. Before the community-based foundation was established in this district, funding was supplied by many outside groups, such as the Gannett Communities Fund. As educators and parents began to see the value of this grant money to children and to the community, they awakened to the possibility of forming their own funding partnerships.

Over the last 6 years, area principals have been encouraged to apply for grants from Nashville's foundation. The grants were first offered to elementary schools and later to middle schools. Typically, written project proposals are reviewed by a committee, which then distributes awards of up to $1,000 per request.

The grant money has been helpful to principals who not only want to involve parents in their student's learning process but also desire to remove any barriers to participation. For example, the awards assist parents who have had difficulty because they live a great distance from the school, have no transportation or child care, or feel they are unable to communicate with school officials.

As a result of Nashville's effective community-based organization, the principals have had even greater opportunities than ever to implement strong home-school ties. For the most part, the principals I work with express a strong commitment to parent involvement in the schools. The following examples recount how these principals have used their grant money to this end.

Project PLUS Is Created

One insightful principal-leader has obtained positive results from monitoring her students' grades every 6 weeks. This practice shows exactly which students need help, what kind of help is needed, and whether there has been progress since the last observation period.

After noticing that certain students were consistently earning Fs, this principal began working with parents and home-based teachers to investigate what causes students to fail. Together they took a creative approach to assist parents in helping children make better grades. Thus Project PLUS (Parents Lifting Up Students) was born.

How It Works

Every 6 weeks, Project PLUS invites parents of students with a failing grade to attend improvement sessions with their child. A written agreement between each parent and child is signed at the beginning of the project. Then parents begin to actively participate in learning at school. The subjects include time management, study skills, individual learning styles, how to be successful in school and ways that parents can help. The foundation grant makes it possible to pay teachers a small fee.

Sessions are held from 6 p.m. to 7 p.m. on Tuesday evenings. At the end of the 6-week period, report cards are monitored again. If students have upgraded to at least a D, they are invited to a pizza party, made possible through a fund especially for this purpose. The student certificates signed at the beginning of the session are awarded along with congratulatory ribbons to let students know how pleased the school staff is with their success. Children have the opportunity to see what can happen when they pull together, forming bonds and learning as a team.

All types and configurations of families attend: fathers and daughters; mothers and sons; fathers, mothers, sons, and daughters. One student's entire family came to school—the mom and dad, the student who received the F, as well as a younger brother and sister. Another family unit made the occasion a "family affair." Following every session, they went out for dinner together as a direct result of attending Project PLUS.

The Positive Results

The principal wanted to know how many students had to repeat a grade level. In 1990, eight students had been retained. The very first year after receiving the grant, only five students were kept back. The next year, there were three; and by 1993, not a single student was retained, all as a direct result of Project PLUS. Report cards indicate when a child is a "graduate." One child who participated even became an honor roll student.

Parents and Teachers Connecting for Kids

In 1993, an elementary school was awarded a $1,000 grant to implement the Parents and Teachers Connecting for Kids project. Because some parents live in inner-city neighborhoods located 32 miles from school, the coprincipals asked for funds to overcome invisible barriers caused by this situation. In their outreach program, school buses pick up parents for a 45-minute ride to visit the school. In addition, faculty members travel to the distant neighborhoods to meet with parents at a local school in the community.

When special programs are scheduled, the school buses are available for all parents who wish to attend. The cost to charter a bus is presently $50 per round trip, regardless of how many parents are on board. Sometimes there have been fewer than 15 parents per trip, and once there was only a mother and her preschooler. Nevertheless, both principals feel this outreach is necessary for effective communication with the parents in that area.

Finding Out Needs

The Parent Involvement Committee at this school decided to focus on how parent involvement could be improved even more. Through a shared leadership decision-making process—involving a council of parents, a community leader, staff, and teacher representatives—they launched a schoolwide effort to address student concerns in four major areas:

1. Student achievement
2. Discipline
3. Multicultural implications
4. Parent involvement

The committee especially wanted to assist the inner-city parents. A second-grade teacher at the school suggested that she survey such parents to assess their needs. The parents were asked to fill out a questionnaire about transportation, child care, time of involvement, their concerns, and what subjects were of interest. After conducting the survey, the teacher said, "I talked with parents who had a genuine interest in their children's educational process. They were happy to help. One parent asked if we could help find her a job. Another parent asked for assistance in helping her child be a better student."

Help Sessions

The information in the survey convinced the grant foundation to award another $1,000. The expanded outreach program was designed to

- Provide training classes for families
- Develop more effective communication between school and home
- Help faculty, parents, and staff to become aware of community agencies able to support families

The additional funding was used to involve community experts in "help sessions" for parents and teachers. Some of the workshops were meant to assist special students, for example those with attention deficit disorders, behavioral problems (including violent behavior), and drug addictions. Other workshops were on topics of general interest, such as family math, conflict resolution, or multicultural education.

Walking the Neighborhood

The grant money was also used to implement an intensive inner-city neighborhood outreach on the part of the school. The principals sent letters to the inner-city parents to let them know they would be at their homes one Monday at 8:30 a.m. They formed teams of teachers, with each team visiting families on several streets. Although they woke up some of the parents and students, there were other parents, grandparents, uncles, and students waiting in their yards for their special visitors!

A teacher commented that at first she was apprehensive about walking the neighborhood. After the visit was over, the teacher said, "It was a good experience for them and for me." Another teacher was eager to make a positive impression on students, parents, and others she visited. She said to them, "We may be across town, but we are still interested in you and your neighborhood."

Each school must decide what is appropriate for its outreach plan. In the Resources section at the end of this book, there is a summary of this school's 1993-1994 parent involvement program that you can use to get started.

Parents Do Care

As parent-consultant, I received a call from an elementary principal requesting help to involve parents. I was able to share with a teacher, a parent, and the principal how parents are lifesavers in education. The student population at this school is under 150, one of the lowest in the district. Just the same, the principal wrote a grant proposal and was awarded $500 to encourage parent involvement. With the money, the school was able to provide child care, door prizes, and refreshments at school functions as well as lunches for parent volunteers.

Say It With a Wish List

I explained how we had used the wish list at Napier to communicate our needs to parents and community members. The principal immediately developed a wish list request form, which was filled out by all the teachers. Soon thereafter, I was asked to speak to the parents at one of the school's Saturday morning gatherings. (These meetings had been instigated by the principal, but the parents chose the day and time to meet.) A sample letter inviting parents to such a meeting is included in the Resources section at the end of this book.

As I entered the school building, I saw several banners on display with the "Parents Are Lifesavers" motto. The principal greeted the parents and shared the vision of having them as partners in students' education. Then she read the teachers' wish list.

There was an overwhelming response! Parents signed up for all types of committees, to work in teachers' rooms, to work on projects at home, and to donate items. One teacher received all but one item on her wish list. One wish was to have a computer. A parent who worked at IBM made this request known to the company officials, and the school soon received a brand new, free IBM computer package. An enthusiastic fourth-grade teacher said it best, "The wish list makes my job so much easier. Students know that their parents are interested in what goes on in the classroom."

I Can Work at Home

One grandmother said, "I can't come to the school, but I can do lots of things at home. I can collect the Lesson Line cards from parents. And if I'm provided with a list of parents who haven't returned theirs, I can make telephone calls to remind them."

Lesson Line is a communication voice mailbox used by some schools in Tennessee. It is a school-to-home communication tool donated by First Tennessee Bank in partnership with *The Tennessean* newspaper. Parents are encouraged to call daily to see if their child has homework or to learn of special events taking place at the school.

A contest was created in 1993 by the First Tennessee Bank and *The Tennessean* to see what parents used the Lesson Line. The school that had the most calls by parents received $500 and an ice cream party for parents. Even though it is one of the smallest, this school won twice within the school year. That achievement came about largely due to the grandmother who organized the cards and called parents!

Parents on Your Side

In March of 1992, I went to conduct a faculty in-service on Parents Are Lifesavers for an urban, but not an inner-city, African American middle school. Most children at the school live in the neighborhood; however, some students are bused in from the suburbs.

When I visited the school, I was met with enthusiasm, and we all enjoyed a wonderful brainstorming session. There were many teachers who seemed willing to go the extra mile to help create the environment needed to encourage parent involvement in their middle school.

A Positive New Image

The apparent problem of this urban school was that teachers and administrative staff were experiencing the repercussions of a negative school image. Many of the parents in the suburbs did not have a favorable opinion of the school.

During the in-service, I said, "You need to get together and decide if you really want parental and community involvement." I then listed a few ideas to give them a starting point:

- Take your message to the community in the suburbs. Inform them of the good things going on at your school.
- Find a way to get a favorable mention in the local newspapers.
- Go to the PTA meetings of your feeder school in the suburbs, before the students attend middle school.
- Write to the churches in both areas. Ask parents and community members to support the school.

I worked with the group, and we were able to accomplish these tasks. It really worked!

Parents Are Invited to Participate

In April 1993, there was an article in the suburban paper about the middle school and who would be attending in the fall. Faculty members became very active, attending PTA meetings in the community of the feeder schools as well as arranging a potluck dinner there to make sure incoming students felt welcome. The student council also visited the elementary schools. The principal, faculty, and staff were excited. A new image was emerging!

When I explained the foundation grant program to the principal, he applied and was awarded $995. Workshops were then planned for the new school year on the theme "Parents on Your Side." Parents were sent an invitation to visit 2 weeks before school started, and an invitation to the suburban community appeared in the local paper. The school administration emphasized the occasion with "Parents Are Lifesavers" T-shirts for the entire faculty and staff, who wore the shirts during the event.

More than 100 parents attended this program, which featured a series of videos on how to assist children with their homework. Reporters from local papers showed up. The parents were enthusiastic.

One parent told the principal that she had already enrolled her child in a private school. She said, "But I'm bringing my child here. A friend has her child registered for a private school, too; I'm going to tell her about the experience here today."

After the program, parents came in and immediately started signing up for committees and volunteering for various projects. So many parents volunteered that the principal asked the vision teacher to move out of her room and into a portable classroom to make room for them.

This empowered faculty bonded with its parents to open a line of communication between the home and school. As a result, the parents felt free to enter the school and assist all teachers. There will always be struggles and obstacles to contend with; but principals, faculty members, and staff members must start somewhere. Don't get hung up on the barriers. Start today and you will benefit the entire learning community.

Establishing a Parent-Volunteer Program

I was asked to conduct another "Parents Are Lifesavers" workshop and help establish a parent-volunteer program at a nearby elementary school. The principal had been receiving a $1,000 foundation grant for the past several years and was eager to facilitate a more organized effort.

The parents wished to create a volunteer handbook covering school needs and job descriptions. They also wanted to set up a center at their open house to display materials on parenting that could be checked out by parents during the school year. The parenting materials were purchased with foundation funds. The program was very successful, and a volunteer handbook was published.

Parents were asked to participate in a volunteer network. A letter was sent home on astrobrite-Mars-magenta-colored fluorescent paper so that parents would be sure to see the important invitation to be a volunteer. Parents answered the call to serve. Many worked on make-and-take projects at the school, and others who were unable to participate on a daily basis assembled packets for these workshops. A sample budget, including materials and equipment for such a parent-involvement program, can be found in the Resources section at the end of this book.

As indicated by the preceding examples, the Metropolitan Nashville Public Education Foundation has been a strong community organization in support of parent involvement within Nashville's public schools. The funds distributed to principals over the last 6 years have succeeded in increasing parent-educator interaction for the benefit of children's learning. Most important, the grants have empowered principals to remove some of the negative barriers hindering the educational process. In the next chapter, you will learn how the ideas discussed so far become even more powerful as they are taken out into the community at large.

6 Educators, Parents, and Community Involvement— It Works! It Works! It Works!

Overcoming Violence in the Schools

In the last few years, the presence of gangs, drugs, and guns in our schools has become a serious problem. Violence is the number one concern of most educators and parents. Recently, in my own area, a 13-year-old child was accidentally shot and killed in class by a classmate. This type of incident has compelled educators, parents, and community members to become united in dealing with safety in the schools.

Many parents have come forward to answer the wake-up alarm caused by the school crisis. Concerned individuals have volunteered to be present on campus and on buses in an effort to curb the violence. Partnerships with the media are helping to educate the public, teaching every citizen how to be a proactive voice for schools.

It took an open-minded administration in Nashville for public schools to open their doors. Now that they are involved, the schools in this system have explored ways to organize volunteers, keep them involved, and to get more people involved. Director of Schools Dr. Richard C. Benjamin and Nashville's mayor, Phil Bredesen, have come up with a five-point program to deal with violence. Two of those points ask for (a) a volunteer network—educators, parents, and student involvement—and (b) students to report other students who have weapons. This chapter will illustrate how by working together, parents have become a voice for reform in Nashville's public schools.

Voices for Reform:
By Sherry Reynolds

When I became the president of Nashville's Parents for Public Education in 1992, one of my main concerns was for the creation of some new magnet schools. Once before, I had worked with parents for an entire year trying to start a magnet school. It was a slow process, but we did get the public stimulated and interested. As a result, the school board decided to appoint a committee to study the possibility of adding some magnet schools. When the list of appointees went to the board for approval, there were no parents on it. I was furious.

Getting the Message Across

Many a parent has discovered that "getting the boss's ear" is not easy. It may be possible once or twice, but administrators are very busy people. They get tons of phone calls from all sorts of irate parents. They get mountains of mail. The fax machine spits out endless memos, and there are always gaggles of people around them before and after meetings.

How can you tell a busy person you are "mad as hell!"? One must be creative. My solution was balloons. I baked a delicious loaf of homemade cinnamon raisin bread and tied to it a bouquet of pink and black helium-filled balloons streaming with pink ribbons. I then tied an irate note to the bouquet, addressed to Dr. Richard C. Benjamin, the school director. In my note, I asked him why parents had not been appointed to the magnet steering committee. I hand delivered the package to the director's office.

It worked. I got a phone call. The administration also sent several letters out to various community organizations and businesses and recruited more members for the committee. Several more people became a part of the decision-making process. Because of my own intense involvement in public schools over 4 years, I had jokingly introduced myself as an "unpaid lobbyist for metro schools."

But eventually, parents who do become involved, committed, and knowledgeable can take a step beyond lobbying the politicians.

Running for Political Office

Parents can get into the political ball game. Many parents run for political office, such as a seat on the school board. In the case of Nashville, the funding body is metro government; so in 1991, I decided to run for one of the five metro council-at-large positions.

I didn't win—I came in ninth, with 17,000 votes. But I did get my message across. I was a single-issue candidate—schools! Among the most stressful parts of a political campaign are the interviews conducted by labor unions, real estate boards, political caucuses, and anyone else who decides to get together to ask candidates a bunch of questions. It is an opportunity like no other, however, to inform influential groups about the realities of the schoolhouse.

My most difficult and stressful interview was with the editorial board of Nashville's largest daily newspaper. I feel that the information I provided was a real eye-opener, however, in that it was presented from a new perspective—that of a parent. It was honest, and I believe it had a positive effect.

Becoming Knowledgeable

Not every parent has the time or inclination to run for the school board or to organize a grassroots organization. Nevertheless, any parent can make a difference. And if the effort is to become more informed, that knowledge can be converted into power. I started my learning process by reading the newspaper daily. Over a 4-year period, I clipped, saved, and read 15 large notebooks full of articles about schools. Reading the paper or listening carefully to the news is a good start.

Asking questions and making phone calls is also easy to do. Public schools are accountable to the public, and those who work for the schools are generally more than happy to answer questions. Knowledge can lead to creative ways to solve problems and help make schools a better place for our children. Informed parents can work wonders.

Teachers, administrators, and school employees have a vested interest in the schools—they work for the system in some way. As parents, we have an even more critical interest—our children. To-gether, we can fight for them; we can speak out for them. We can say what the teachers and the administrators can't say. We can't get fired. We don't have to worry about a raise or promotion. We are parents for life, and we can make a difference. Let's hope that the real "political parent power potential" is someday realized. Parents, let's get involved today for the children and the future of public schools.

Parents for Public Education (PPE) in Nashville is still ongoing. In addition, PPE is now teaming up with the "Parents Are Life-savers" program.

Working Together for Reform: The Story of BURNT

Some parents feel their responsibility to children stops with the raising of their own children, that they are not directly responsible for others. This is the view that "our family is an island."

"Much can be accomplished by working as individual parents. But no family functions in isolation from the rest of society. We are all dependent on the community for our existence. Working in groups can make a big difference toward improving the commu-nity," says Nancy McFadden.

A mother of two, Nancy McFadden has worked and researched for the past 6 years on issues of pesticide reform. She learned a lot working as an individual but has made the most significant positive changes through being a member of BURNT (Bring Urban Recycling to Nashville Today), an effective nonprofit environmental group.

According to Nancy,

> One strength of groups is the power of consultation. When a group works together on an issue, each member brings an individual perspective. Viewing issues from several perspectives and sharing those perspectives moves us closer to the best solution—and provides for more effective work.
>
> Second, groups share responsibility. Some of us have strengths in fund-raising, secretarial work, or bookkeeping, while others lobby officials, make phone calls, enjoy public speaking, tutor children, or use their writing talent. When one person cannot

attend a meeting, another one can. Not one of us is capable of doing alone all the work that needs to be done to make the world better for our children.

Third, working with others provides a social support system. We have all experienced rejection. There are times we work so hard to get a concept across only to have a decision maker say, "But this is the real world. We can't do this" and decide to steadfastly ignore the issue. That is when we need other people with whom we agree—to talk to, to help us refine our viewpoint, and to work with us. We help each other recharge so we can get back to work again. Together, we can see the progress we have made and acknowledge our accomplishments. (personal interview)

Perseverance Leads the Way

Three years ago, BURNT started an urban pesticide use reduction campaign. Schools were targeted. Because children in schools cannot leave freely and are dependent on adults, they needed protection first. BURNT, working with the National Coalition Against the Misuse of Pesticides, collected information on successful alternatives and pesticide dangers. They gathered the bad news about the casual use of pesticides by Metro Nashville's pest control contractor. They gathered the good news about an alternative called integrated pest management (IPM), already in use in progressive school systems and at the National Park Service, among other agencies.

BURNT put together the research and presented that information to government officials responsible for children. Although there was not immediate agreement regarding pesticide dangers and the advantages of using fewer pesticides, BURNT persevered with letters and phone calls. Over a 7-month period, BURNT had left a noticeable paper trail on the issue of pesticides in Metropolitan Nashville Public Schools.

Help From the Media

BURNT had learned from earlier work on solid waste how to interest the press in a story. In February 1992, an excellent BURNT press conference was broadcast over local news stations for 2 days and was published in detail in both papers. When pesticide alternatives were presented to the Metro School Board 2 days later, board members were eager to hear the alternative.

The coverage by the media helped to convince school board members that they needed to pay attention. BURNT then worked with school employees to help design a safer, more effective pest management program, finding good resources nationwide. To their credit, Metro employees were willing and able to learn new techniques and ideas. We continue to work with them to refine the program.

A Team Approach

In the summer of 1993, BURNT and Metro Nashville Schools jointly held an IPM workshop with leaders from the International Pest Management Institute (IPMI). This well-attended workshop trained Metro custodians and staff in IPM, which entails better maintenance of grounds, keeping food and water away from pests, and using less toxic pesticides and only when necessary. Recertification points for licensed pest control operators were offered through the University of Tennessee.

The Plan Comes Alive

In the summer of 1994, after receiving more information from BURNT, the Nashville public schools adopted the first posting policy in Tennessee. As of that August, if pesticides were to be used, a sign had to be posted to warn parents and children and to prevent any unnecessary exposure. Information sheets on pesticides must be kept in every school office. Less toxic methods are encouraged, and no pesticides are ever to be used while children are at school.

In the last 2 years, the Nashville system has made good progress on IPM and pesticide use reduction. BURNT continues to provide new information and resources as they are made available while holding Metro accountable for further progress. As more citizens become informed of the dangers of pesticides, BURNT plans to encourage that awareness. Metro's continuous progress and BURNT's long-term encouragement and gentle pressure exemplify how groups are accomplishing much together.

According to Nancy McFadden,

> The power of assertive, informed citizens working in groups is
> amazing. If we work together as parents and as a community, we
> can change the world into a place that is safe for all of our children.
> In addition, we will give our children a great message—that
> positive social change is possible, that problems are solvable if
> people of goodwill work on them in groups. If we give our chil-
> dren a safer environment and hope that change is possible, we will
> give them better hope for their own futures. (personal interview)

See the Resources section at the end of this book for names and
addresses of groups concerned with the safer use of pesticides and
with successful alternatives.

An Entire Community Responds to a Crisis

Lorraine B. Wallach (1994) has written a piece for the *ERIC Digest
on Violence and Young Children's Development*. She describes violence
as a learned behavior that must be changed. Acts of violence that
families are exposed to are listed by Ms. Wallach: child abuse; family
conflict; gang activity; neighborhood crime, such as murder, the sale
and use of drugs, and robbery; and emotional, psychological, and
mental danger.

Many children in the world live in an unhealthy environment.
They bring the repercussions of violent behavior and frustration to
the classroom, playground, bus stop, and bus. Violence knows no
boundaries, experts say. Even when children reside in a home where
stable values are taught, they are still confronted with the perils of
today's society.

A Wake-Up Call

In 1994, a child in a wheelchair shattered our idea of the stereotypical child with a disability when he took his mom's gun to a
Nashville school. The student said it was for protection. He showed
the gun to another student while the class watched a video in a
darkened classroom. The second student was playing with the gun

when it went off, the bullet hitting a third student in the head. The injured student was pronounced dead before he could get medical attention.

The middle school where the casualty with death took place is located in an affluent community where most parents are well educated and can afford the best for their children. The day this casualty occurred, parents expressed their fears, concerns, and rage. They were afraid to learn of the child's identity, terrified at the thought that it might be their own child. Parents called the central office and jammed every phone line. The media were given a play-by-play description of the accident, detailing how the child lost his life while attending a public school.

The entire Nashville community, as well as the state of Tennessee, was extremely upset over this incident. The mayor and other high-profile elected officials, along with all central office administrators from the Board of Education, arrived on the crime scene immediately to give assistance. Guidance counselors and social workers from the system were called on and given instruction to help parents and students. They listened as students expressed their anxieties and fears of returning to school. Parents were not allowed to go into the school building, and students could not come out until the gun was found.

The Media Assist Volunteers

A Nashville radio station joined a local television station to sponsor a volunteer phone line. It played a recorded message for those persons in the community who had questions or concerns. Many wanted to volunteer to help provide a safer environment for public schools. Volunteers included YMCA personnel, senior citizens, single adults, college students, ministers, elected officials, and concerned citizens.

As parent consultant, I was able to organize the volunteers and return phone calls on behalf of Dr. Richard Benjamin. We placed over 200 volunteers in schools. The media kept up with the report on a weekly basis, giving details of positive news. Some of those who were already volunteering called the Volunteer Network to encourage the director and school personnel. People said, "I want to go where I can help. I want to go to a middle or high school."

The presence of extra adults in the public schools reassured students and educators who were afraid. In addition, adult volunteers saw exactly what teachers face and endure on a daily basis. At first, some students resisted the policing of their turf. But Dr. Benjamin, along with school principals, kept speaking to the adults, saying, "You are welcome to help." Soon, more adults accepted the open invitation, answering the wake-up call to work toward providing a safer school environment.

Student Information Hotline

The mayor installed toll-free telephones in each middle and high school for students to report *any* student who has a weapon. Now, each caller is rewarded with $500 for information resulting in an arrest. Students are warned not to take any replica of a weapon into cars, the bus, or the school. Lockers can be searched at any time, according to the discretion of local school officials. The new school year of 1994 called for zero tolerance of weapons. If a student is caught with either a replica or a real weapon, this individual is to be suspended to an alternative school for a year.

The family of the student who died expressed the wish that his death not be in vain. They hope this tragedy will serve as a "wake-up call." Educators, parents, and community members have joined together in each public school in Nashville to develop a health and safety plan. Everyone has been educated about the fact that weapons have no place in children's learning.

Parent Presence in Halls, in Lunchrooms, and on Buses

In another Nashville elementary school, a principal applied for a community-based foundation grant and was awarded $1,000 to feed parent volunteers breakfast and lunch. The volunteers were there to monitor halls, patrol the lunchroom, and ride the school bus to and from the inner city.

To facilitate communication, an orientation was held with bus transportation supervisors, the PTO president, the principal, and myself. The next day, an orientation was held for the volunteers who learned important information about the school personnel's expectations for safety. The parents voiced concerns about issues such as (a) the fights that occur before the bus arrives—who handles the problem? (b) older students bullying younger students; (c) students going to a nearby store before the bus arrives, making the bus driver wait for them; (d) lack of respect students have for adults and other students; and (e) transportation problems when going back home. Administrators and the PTO president were willing to listen to parents' concerns and came up with solutions.

Two weeks into the new school year, this principal reported that the parents' presence provided a change in the attitude of students. He felt it had been worth the time and effort invested. The volunteering parents were given free breakfast and lunch in appreciation of their much needed assistance.

Effective Models of School-Parent Relationships

Using parent's expertise in any school organization or committee is vital to the success of the programs. Educators are so used to parents playing an inactive role in decision-making processes that many parents are excluded, not because they are not wanted but because no one at the school was in the habit of including them.

Principals, involve your students, parents, teachers, and community members in building safer and stronger schools. Two of the eight major goals of the U.S. Department of Education are (a) making schools safe and drug free, an effort that must involve the entire community, and (b) promoting parental involvement in every school across America in the hope of helping students reach their educational goals and prepare them to be successful in schools, in the workplace, and in this global society.

One inner-city high school had such a negative reputation that the administration, staff, and students (but no parents) implemented a Drug Free, Weapon Free, and Violence Free program. The program began with staff development for staff members in conflict mediation and cultural program diversity. To curb violence, a peer conflict mediation program for students was implemented to help students learn to handle anger and conflict. Violent incidents decreased 50% with the peer mediation program implementation.

Nevertheless, after a major altercation at the school, which received local and national media attention, over 300 educators, parents, students, and other concerned citizens met at a local church. The academic climate of the school was in need of an overhaul, which was immediately noticed by all who attended the meeting. Parents and community members responded to the wake-up call and formed a Concerned Parents' Network at the meeting. Every time the Concerned Parents' Network had a meeting, they informed the media about the problems and solutions that would be discussed at the meeting. Most parents and students wanted to know what had to be done to be assured that the school was a safe place.

The principal asked for parents to walk the halls daily in pairs—an African American parent and a Caucasian parent. He also invited ministers from local churches to a community luncheon to request assistance in getting parents involved. Because the principal extended the welcome to parents to become partners in the school, parents continue to walk the halls and help curb the violence at the school.

For the parents to become proactive voices for reform, the school's assistant principal began holding problem-solving classes for parents to voice their input. Parents voted that the most pressing problems at the school included the following:

- Isolation of problem students
- Stricter discipline
- More teacher control in the classrooms
- Rules applicable to all students
- More security in the school parking lot

Among other successes, the parents and staff established a new tardy policy, reduced the student open displays of affection in the halls, and succeeded in pressuring the district to repair the 56 door locks on the exterior of the school, which had been broken for some time despite repeated repair requests from the school.

The Concerned Parents' Network has been a success because of the motivation of parents and the efforts of the principal, who could have said, "We [the staff] can handle this problem ourselves."

Instead, he reached out to parents, and the community used its talents and proactive voices. He gave the parents the opportunity to voice their opinions. He listened to what they had to say and put their ideas into practice. He listened not only with his head but with his heart. The high school principal made it easier for his parents to become partners in the education of their children.

Dr. Richard Benjamin's Mission for Parents

When Dr. Richard Benjamin speaks his concerns to educators and media representatives about parent involvement, his words are clear: "We're not going to get where we want to go with students' achievement without creating strong partnerships with parents and families."

According to Dr. Benjamin, this ranges all the way from delivering the invitation for parents to become involved to going where parents are to encourage them to become involved—in fact, mandating parent involvement through school improvement plans. For example, he has worked with the juvenile court to instigate policies sentencing parents of juvenile offenders to ride buses or attend classrooms where students have been disruptive.

Parents know that this board is serious! They will remove barriers for parents who want to become involved. It's ironic that on one hand there are people who want to be involved but aren't able to for a variety of reasons or who may not feel welcome. On the other hand, some people truly don't want to be involved and must be sentenced by the court system to get their participation.

Handling Teen Violence

During an interview, Dr. Benjamin declared that it is essential for parents to get involved; and when they are willing, we have to make it easy for them. *The Tennessean* featured Dr. Benjamin and asked how he would handle teen violence. He responded, "This may sound funny, but I wouldn't spend it [money] on teens. I'd spend it on K through fourth grades—to create a partnership between teachers and parents to work together to develop good character early."

Dr. Benjamin continued:

If you have Band-Aid programs at middle schools and high schools with violent kids, you're going to have those problems forever. But if you partner with parents to instill good ethical values early on, then you have a chance to avoid the problems with prevention. In instilling values early on, this means working carefully with parents in the program. (unpublished interview)

Plans for Project Solution

In order to help the partnership between parents and schools, *The Tennessean* agreed to publish a supplement every two weeks so that students and parents could work on the same character trait being emphasized at school at the same time. *The Tennessean* formed a partnership with the Metropolitan Nashville Public Schools system at the cost of $750,000 over a 5-year period. The Newspapers in Education Department of the paper, along with teachers and administrators, developed lessons and activities for grades K through four. The eight-page lessons are printed daily, although teachers are not required to use them. Because the lessons are so readily accessible, we have found many parents using and appreciating this free resource.

In addition, parents and teachers have created a resource team to teach young students values for life. The 18 traits included in the character education program are as follows:

- Respects self
- Does what is right
- Respects others
- Accepts responsibility
- Builds community
- Cares
- Nurtures family members and friends
- Loves learning
- Takes initiative
- Models democratic ideals and practices
- Forgives
- Practices honesty

- Perseveres
- Demonstrates gratitude
- Demonstrates courage
- Gives services
- Respects work

Dr. David Jones, Jr., Metro Assistant Superintendent, Curriculum and Instruction, was quoted in the September 1994 issue of *The Tennessean:*

> We must make students aware that there are universal principles that guide us and bind us together as humans. Values that transcend geography, transcend ethnicity, and transcend religion— that's what makes us human. We will see, as a result, a population kinder, more sensitive, and less hostile. (Long, 1994, p. 3b)

Conclusion

It has been a heartfelt privilege to have this opportunity to bring these experiences to you. As you can see, educators, parents, and the community have real-life concerns. We, as adults, need to be effective role models for children. They should see their parents talking and acting in positive ways—especially in their own homes. Too often, schools and community organizations are the most positive places students have—the only place a mentor might say, "I care."

Parents, go to the schools and give of your time and energies— not only for your own child but for other students, too. Be on the lookout for students who need the extra attention that only you can give. Walk the halls, ride the buses to and from school, and monitor the lunchroom. You have the extra time and voice to create positive reform and change for the benefit of a child.

Educators, I have heard parents voice their frustrations and concerns daily. Utilize these parents. Listen to them. Make them lifesavers in public education today. Educators, parents, and community involvement—It works! It works! It works!

Resources

From Chapter 2

Survey to Assess the School's Climate

1. What do you like about the physical surroundings of our school?

2. How would you like to see the physical surroundings of our school changed or improved?

3. How would you rate the "warmth factor" of our faculty and staff?

1	2	3	4	5
Cold		Indifferent		Friendly
Unsmiling		Lukewarm		Welcoming
Distant				Concerned
No eye contact				

4. What suggestions have you wanted to make for the improvement of the school?

5. How would you rate the unity of our school?

1	2	3	4	5
Not united				Very united

6. What obstacles, if any, hinder your involvement in our school?

7. How can faculty members and the principal facilitate more parental involvement at our school?

8. How easy is it to talk to your child's teacher?

1	2	3	4	5
Very hard				Very easy

9. How easy is it to talk to the principal?

1	2	3	4	5
Very hard				Very easy

10. How welcome are you made to feel by each of the following?

The principal

1	2	3	4	5
Very unwelcome				Very welcome

Your child's teacher

1	2	3	4	5
Very unwelcome				Very welcome

The school's staff members

1	2	3	4	5
Very unwelcome				Very welcome

From Chapter 3

Job Description of a Volunteer

Job Title: Tutor

Mission: Help students Kindergarten through 12th grade on a one-to-one basis. Subjects include everyday skills, reading, math, or English.

Qualifications: A volunteer who has sensitivity, a high school education, and good communication skills and who loves children.

Time: 1 hour per week

Place: Acme High School

Orientation: You may attend an orientation planned by the district (Sept. 8, 1995) or visit your local school (Oct. 1, 1995).

The volunteer will meet with the principal or volunteer coordinator once a month to discuss progress and to ensure a commitment to the task.

Parents' Volunteer Enlistment Form

We are glad you have an interest in our school.

Name: _____

Street Address: _____

City: _____Zip: _____

Phone: _____(home) _____(office)

Volunteer experience:

Talents and hobbies:

Education:

Current occupation:

Talents, hobbies, skills:

In what type of volunteer opportunities are you interested?

A. Working with children

B. Library

C. Preparing materials

D. Clerical

E. Schoolwide

What times are you available?

A. Morning

B. Afternoons

C. Night (evenings)

D. Saturday or Sunday

List name, address, and phone number of three personal references:

_____

_____

_____

Please return this volunteer enlistment form to the principal's office or to the volunteer coordinator's mailbox.

Request for Parents' Help

Dear Friend:

I would first like to begin by introducing myself. My name is

_____,
president of the PTA at _____
Middle School. I have a son who attends the school; this is to be his second
year. I have an older son who also attended. My husband's name is

_____,
and we are concerned and dedicated parents, determined to help support
and educate our children, all of the children, in any way that we can.

Our school is located at _____.
This inner-city school is in a very low-income area. Parents, faculty, and
staff have but one goal—to build the self-esteem of, and give a sense of
responsibility and accomplishment to, the young people who attend this
school. They deserve a chance to believe in not only themselves but in
something to make them proud. We want and strive for that something to
be their school. This is only the beginning—and what an impression this
would make.

We, the school family, are asking you to help us meet our goals. We
are going to need a lot of help. Contributions of any kind would be greatly
appreciated. Paper, pencils, pens, paint, glue, posters, markers, cookies,
candy, soft drinks, punch, radios, tape players, software, and diskettes are
some of the items used on a daily basis and that are always needed.

In closing, on behalf of the principal, faculty, staff, and the whole
school family, we ask you to help us in any way that you can. A most
sincere thank-you in advance for your kind help and consideration. I look
forward to hearing from you. Please do not hesitate to contact me with any
questions.

Sincerely yours,

President, PTA

Invitation to Parent-Teacher Club

Dear Parents:

Our membership drive has begun. It will extend through _____ Open House—October 8, 1995. The membership dues are $1.00 or more. We have sent home a volunteer interest form, membership letter, and printed envelopes. Please place your dues in the printed envelopes. Our goal for the Parent/Teacher Club membership drive is to reach 100% participation in each classroom. Sometime in October, the PTC will provide *all* classrooms with a special treat. Anyone who cares about our children can join (grandparents, aunts, uncles, friends, and neighbors).

The club is organized to support teachers as they help children become successful. Money raised last year was used to purchase items on the teachers' "wish list" and for the benefit of the school. The money this year, set by the Plan to Action Team, will be used for media center equipment, field trips, and Jelly Bean Fun Day. The PTC also helps the school pay for a leased copy machine at $70.00 per month.

Last year's club was a big success because of the principal, staff, parents, and community supporters.

Just a note: The PTC completed a wish list for all teachers last year. It was a team effort that was successful. We will send a wish list home soon. Please help us grant our teachers' wishes by providing the items on their lists to show our support.

Open House is October 8, 1995, at 7:00 p.m. We will sell _____ School T-shirts and bags, and we will serve refreshments. We do not believe in having our students sell door-to-door. We have created other ways to help fill our needs.

For example, we sponsor a "general store," a small store set up on stage one Friday each month. Children buy tickets before schools starts for 25¢ each. These tickets can then be used to purchase items such as a used dress, a cupcake, or a toy. The children also learn independence by making choices and paying for tickets. Parent volunteers are there to help children with their purchases and take them back to classrooms. The PTC asks parents to donate baked goods, old toys, clothing, and books. Just send to school in a bag marked "General Store." Parents, we need you.

Some of the proceeds from the general store will be used for the teachers' wish list. Thanks again for your support.

President, Parent/Teacher Club

From Chapter 4

Parent Involvement Opportunities

Dear Parent:

Every child needs a friend or two or three. Would you like to volunteer? You don't have to be a professional. You can even do some jobs at home! A "volunteer" is someone who, along with the teacher, helps a child believe in himself or herself. We provide orientation and training for all volunteers.

If you would like to be a volunteer, please check below where you could provide assistance. Plans for orientation will be coming soon.

☐ Work with children

☐ Help with art activities

☐ Read stories

☐ Help in learning centers

☐ Tutor individual children or small groups

☐ Help with dramatic rehearsals

☐ Help with vision examinations

☐ Help children make and put up bulletin boards

☐ Help with a field day

☐ Help as lunch hostess or host

☐ Help students write books

☐ Listen to students read

☐ Act as a computer assistant

☐ Help in the clinic

☐ Be a room parent

☐ Share your native language with students

☐ Help in the library

_____Process paperbacks

_____Work in circulation

☐ Assist with accelerated readers

☐ Prepare materials (at home or school)

☐ Make instructional games and activities

_____ Gather art or instructional supplies

_____ Cut out laminated materials

_____ Audiotape stories and other readings

_____ Take photographs

_____ Make bulletin boards

_____ Check out books on units of study

_____ Translate native languages for non-English-speaking parents

_____ Help with clerical tasks

_____ Run photocopy machine

_____ Help with typing

_____ Help with filing

_____ Call other parents

☐ Schoolwide

_____ Teach workshops

_____ Make and put up bulletin boards

_____ Send party supplies

_____ Help with landscaping

_____ Call parents

_____ Serve on PTA committees

_____ Help with fund-raising

_____ Help with the general store

_____ Contribute to teachers' wish list

_____ Serve on site-based council

_____ Facilitate classroom discussion

_____ Other

Please indicate day and hours you are free to help:

Monday: _____

Tuesday: _____

Wednesday: _____

Thursday: _____

Friday: _____

Are you willing to work with a teacher other than your own child's teacher?

        Yes   No

I am willing to volunteer, but I can only work at home.

Parent's name: _____

Child's name: _____

Phone number: _____

Teacher: _____

If you have any suggestions, please add them here:

_____

_____

_____

_____

_____

From Chapter 5

Parent Activities
of Connecting for Kids

August—Teachers planned a reception at a nearby school. They gave out "goody bags" containing supplies such as pencils, erasers, and so on; served refreshments; and talked with parents.

September—Open house at school; school buses were chartered for the transportation of students and parents. All parents were invited to the school to see school building and to meet with teachers and principals.

October—Parent-Teacher Conference Day. Buses were provided for parents of children in Grades 1 through 3. The fourth-grade team spent half of the day at a school near the neighborhood.

November—PTO meeting to promote PTO excitement and attendance; $25 worth of groceries were awarded as a door prize.

December—Christmas coffee and student program. Buses were chartered to pick up parents who had to travel a great distance.

January—No scheduled activities.

February—Gift certificates for $25 worth of groceries were offered to promote PTO attendance. A bus was provided to transport students and parents to and from a Valentine's Day dance at the school.

March—Gift certificates for $25 worth of groceries were offered to promote PTO attendance.

April—No scheduled activities.

May—Parents provided their own transportation for field day activities.

Parents Do Care:
Classroom Requests

October 18, 1995

Dear Parent:

On Saturday, September 25, parent volunteers met to attend a workshop to discuss ways in which we, as parents, can help our children during their learning years. Lots of ideas were passed along, and each parent seemed eager to help in any way that he or she could. Mrs. Smith solicited requests for specific classroom needs from each teacher and compiled a "wish list." I volunteered as the parent contact for Mrs. Jones's class.

These are some of the items Mrs. Jones could use during this school year:

- ☐ Donation of three rolls of 35 mm film, 24 or 36 exposures and a parent volunteer to have film developed at different times throughout the year

- ☐ Volunteers to allow students to read orally to them once weekly for 30 to 45 minutes

- ☐ Donations from Sam's Wholesale

    ____Jolly Ranchers—1-lb. bag, $12.53

    ____3 × 4 dry erase board, $29.98 (already donated)

    ____Easel for board, $31.43

- ☐ Volunteer to take refreshments (cupcakes and punch) to school for Christmas and Valentine's Day parties

- ☐ Donation of an electric typewriter(s) for a publishing center

- ☐ Volunteer to help students publish books during 4th, 5th, and 6th weeks of the school year

- ☐ Volunteer for the "JUST SAY NO" club meetings. Activities include making baskets, greeting cards, and so on.

- ☐ Seamstress to make chairback covers with pockets to help students keep their supplies organized

I know that many of you are working parents, as I am, but you would still like to contribute to the needs of our children. Whatever you can do will be greatly appreciated. If you are able to volunteer or donate any of the items mentioned above, please call me.

Thanks so much,

Parent Volunteer

Volunteers' Program Budget
for Materials and Equipment

Item	Supplier	Budgeted Amount
Paperbacks for Grades 4 through 6 for book swap	Ingram Book Company	$500.00
Materials for four make-and-take workshops	Metro Warehouse, Acme, Southern School Supply	200.00
Volunteer workshop and handbooks	Acme School Supply	100.00
Parent media materials	Lee Cantor & Associates	300.00

NOTE: PTA pays for programs beyond the $1,000 limit.

From Chapter 6

Groups Concerned With the Safer Use
of Pesticides and Promoting Alternatives

Bring Urban Recycling to Nashville Today
P.O. Box 128555
Nashville, TN 37212
(615) 385-7214
Joyce Vaughn, President

National Coalition Against the Misuse of Pesticides
701 East Street, SE, Suite 200
Washington, DC 20003
(203) 543-5450
Jay Feldman, Executive Director

International Pest Management Institute
P.O. Box 389
Bryans Road, MD 20616
(301) 753-6930
Bill Currie, Director

Parent Involvement Resources

AARP Grandparent Information Center
601 E Street, NW
Washington, DC 20049
(202) 434-2288

Alliance of Involved Parents
P.O. Box 59
East Chatman, NY 12060-0059
(518) 392-6900

Appalachian Educational Laboratory
P.O. Box 1348
Charleston, WV 25325
(304) 347-0400

Association for Childhood Education (ACE I)
11141 Georgia Avenue, Suite 200
Wheaton, MD 20902
(800) 423-3563

Aspira Association
1112 16th Street, NW, Suite 340
Washington, DC 20036
(202) 835-3600

A Better Chance
419 Boylston Street
Boston, MA 02116
(617) 421-0950

Center for Law and Education/NCCE
1875 Connecticut Avenue, Suite 510
Washington, DC 20009

Center for the Study of Parent Involvement
370 Camino Pablo
Orinda, CA 94563
(510) 254-0110

Center on Organization and Restructuring of Schools
Schools of Education—Wisconsin Center for Education Research
University of Wisconsin—Madison
1025 W. Johnson Street
Madison, WI 53706
(608) 263-7575

Children and Fellow
Annie E. Casey Foundation
1225 Martha Custis Drive
Alexandria, VA 22302

Children's Defense Fund
122 C Street, NW, Suite 400
Washington, DC 20001
(202) 628-8787

Citizen's Education Center Parent Leadership Training Project
105 South Main Street
Seattle, WA 98104
(206) 624-9955

Community Programs and Services
701 East Main Street
Lexington, KY 40502
(606) 281-0218

Designs for Change
2205 State, Suite 1900
Chicago, IL 60604
(312) 922-0317

End Violence Against the Next Generation
977 Keeler Avenue
Berkeley, CA 94708-1498
(415) 527-0454

Families Are for Caring
Bailey School
2000 Greenwood
Nashville, TN 37206
(615) 262-6670

Family Resource Coalition
200 S. Michigan Avenue, #1520
Chicago, IL 60604-2404
(312) 341-0900

Family, School, and Community Partnerships Project Office
3200 Coldspring
Indianapolis, IN 46222
(317) 929-0626

Family Service America
1319 F Street, NW, Suite 204
Washington, DC 20004
(202) 347-1124

The Freedom Forum First Amendment
Center at Vanderbilt University
1207 18th Avenue, South
Nashville, TN 37212
(615) 321-9588

HIPPY USA
National Council of Jewish Women
53 West 23rd Street
New York, NY 10010
(212) 645-4048

Hispanic Policy Development Project
250 Park Avenue, South, Suite 5000A
New York, NY 10003
(212) 529-3923

Home and School Institute
1201 16th Street, NW
Washington, DC 20036
(202) 466-3633

Home and School Institute
Mega Skills Education Center
1500 Massachusetts Avenue, NW
Washington, DC 20036-5649
(202) 466-3633

Institute for Educational Leadership
1001 Connecticut Avenue, NW, Suite 310
Washington, DC 20036
(202) 822-8405

Institute for Responsive Education
605 Commonwealth Avenue
Boston, MA 02215
(617) 353-3309

International Child Resource Institute
1810 Hopkins Street
Berkeley, CA 94707
(510) 644-1000

League of Schools Reaching Out
605 Commonwealth Avenue
Boston, MA 02251
(617) 353-3309

MELD
123 North Third Street, Suite 507
Minneapolis, MN 55401
(612) 332-7563

Metropolitan Nashville Public Education Foundation
P.O. Box 50640
Nashville, TN 37205
(615) 383-6773

National Association of Partners in Education
209 Madison Street, Suite 401
Alexandria, VA 22314
(703) 684-4880

National Association of State Boards of Education
1012 Cameron Street
Alexandria, VA 22314
(703) 684-4000

National Coalition Against the Misuse of Pesticides
701 E Street, SE, Suite 200
Washington, DC 2003
(202) 543-5450

National Coalition for Parent Inolvement in Education
P.O. Box 39
1201 16th Street, NW
Washington, DC 20036

National Coalition of Advocates for Students
100 Boylston Street, Suite 737
Boston, MA 02116
(617) 357-8507

National Coalition of Title I/Chapter 1 Parents
9th and D Streets, NE, 2nd Floor
Washington, DC 20002
(202) 547-9266

National Committee for Citizens in Education
900 Second Street, NE, Suite 8
Washington, DC 20002
(202) 408-0447 or 1-800-638-9675

National Crime Prevention Council
Tools to Involve Parents in Gang Prevention
1700 K Street, NW, 2nd Floor
Washington, DC 2006-3817

National Development Office, Parents for Public Schools
3046 Fairfield Avenue
Cincinnati, OH 45206
(513) 221-7773

National Education Association
1201 16th Street, NW
Washington, DC 20036
(202) 822-7015

The National Family Involvement Partnership for Learning
600 Independence Avenue, SW
Washington, DC 20202-8173

National Institute for Multiculture Education
84 Grecian, NW
Albuquerque, NM 87107
(505) 344-6898

National Parent Information Network
University of Illinois at Urbana-Champaign
805 W. Pennsylvania Avenue
Urban, IL 61801-4987
1-800-583-4135

National Parenting Institute
P.O. Box 1252
Temecula, CA 92593
(909) 694-8910

National Resource Center on Family Based Services
University of Iowa, School of Social Work
112 Northhall
Iowa City, IA 52242
(319) 335-2200

National School Volunteer Program
300 N. Washington Street
Alexandria, VA 22314

Parent Involvement Center Chapter 1
Technical Association Center
RMC Research Corporation
400 Lafayette Road
Hampton, NH 03842
(603) 926-8888

Parents and Teachers Against Violence in Education
560 S. Hartz Avenue, Suite 408
Danville, CA 94526
(415) 831-1661

Parents Are Teachers
9374 Olive Blvd.
St. Louis, MO 63132
(314) 432-4330

Parents for Public Education
National Office
P.O. Box 12807
Jackson, MS 39236-2807
(800) 880-1222

Parents of Murdered Children
100 E. 8th Street, Apt. B-41
Cincinnati, OH 45202
(513) 721-5682

Parents Rights Organization
12571 Northwinds Drive
St. Louis, MO 63146
(314) 434-4171

Public Education Fund Network
601 13th Street, NW, Suite 290-N
Washington, DC 20005

Quest International
P.O. Box 566
537 Jones Road
Granville, OH 43023
(614) 522-6450

San Francisco School Volunteers
65 Battery Street, 3rd Floor
San Francisco, CA 94111
(415) 274-0250

Toughlove
P.O. Box 1069
Doylestown, PA 18901
(800) 333-1069

Webster's International, Inc.
5729 Cloverland Place
Brentwood, TN 37027
(800) 727-6833
(615) 373-1723

Youth for Understanding
3501 Newark Street, NW
Washington, DC 20016
(202) 466-6808

References

Barth, R. S. (1990). *Improving schools from within.* San Francisco: Jossey-Bass.

Bolander, D. O., & Stodden, V. L. (Eds.). (1986). *New Webster's dictionary.* New York: Lexicon.

Boyer, E. L. (1991). *Ready to learn: A mandate for the nation.* Princeton, NJ: Carnegie Foundation for the Advancement of Teaching.

Covey, S. R. (1989). *The seven habits of highly effective people.* New York: Simon & Schuster.

Covey, S. R. (1992). *Principle-centered leadership.* New York: Simon & Schuster.

DePree, M. (1989). *Leadership is an art.* New York: Bantam.

Epstein, J. L. (1993, April). Making parents your partners. *Instructor,* pp. 52-53.

Lezotte L. W., & Jacoby, B. C. (1990). *A guide to the school improvement process based on effective school research.* Okemos, MI: Michigan Institute for Educational Management, Effective School Products.

Long, D. (1994, September 5). Growing up right. *The Tennessean,* p. 3b.

Verderber, R. F. (1975). *Communicate.* Belmont, CA: Wadsworth.

Wallach, L. B. (1994, June). *Violence and young children's development* [memo]. (Available from ERIC Clearinghouse on Elementary and Early Childhood Education, University of Illinois, 805 W. Pennsylvania Ave., Urbana, IL 61801-4897; 1-800-583-4135)

Suggested Readings

Bloom, J. (1992). *Parenting our schools.* Boston: Little, Brown.

Burns, R. C. (1993). *Parents and schools: From visitors to partners.* Washington, DC: National Education Association.

Cartisano, J. A. (1993). *A guide to work rules in the New York City public schools.* Collaborative Effort, Educational Priorities Panel, New York. (Available from Educational Priorities Panel, 23 Warren St., 4th Floor, New York, NY 10007)

Church of Jesus Christ of Latter-Day Saints. (1976-1977). *Women's relief society courses of study on delegation* (Lesson 7, Social relations). Salt Lake City, UT: Author.

Curcio, J. L. (1993). *Violence in the schools.* Newbury Park, CA: Corwin.

Frank, M. O. (1986). *How to get your point across in 30 seconds or less.* New York: Simon & Schuster.

Karanberg, S. (1993). *50 important things you can do to improve education.* New York: Book Industry Study Group and National Association of Partners in Education.

National Education Association. (1991). *Bring business and community resources into your classroom.* Washington, DC: Author.

National Schools Volunteer Program, Inc. (1978-1981). *Schools volunteer programs.* Alexandria, VA: Author.

Quarles, C. L. (1993). *Staying safe at school.* Newbury Park, CA: Corwin.

Rich, D. (1992). *Mega skills.* New York: Houghton Mifflin.

Rioux, W. J., & Berla, N. (1993). *Innovations in parent and family involvement.* Princeton Junction, NJ: Eye on Education.

Rotter, J. C., Robinson, E., & Fey, M. (1987). *Parent/teacher conferencing* (NEA Professional Library). Washington, DC: National Education Association.

Shelton, M., & Bauer, L. (1994). *Secrets of highly effective meetings.* Thousand Oaks, CA: Corwin.

Swap, S. M. (1990). *Parent involvement and success for all.* Boston: Institute for Responsive Education.

Warner, C. (1994). *Promoting your school.* Thousand Oaks, CA: Corwin.

Wheeler, M. B. (1986). *The basic meeting manual.* Nashville, TN: Thomas Nelson.

White, R., & Lippitt, R. (1968). Leader behavior and member reaction: Three "social climates." In D. Cartwright & A. Zonder (Eds.), *Group dynamics* (3rd ed.). New York: Harper & Row.